RICHARD BEWES

THE
STONE
THAT BECAME A
MOUNTAIN

Getting it RIGHT about the Kingdom of God

Christian Focus Publications

ISBN 1-85792-714-1

Published in 2001
by
Christian Focus Publication, Geanies House, Fearn,
Ross-shire, IV20 1TW, Great Britain.

www.christianfocus.com

Previously published as *Does God Reign?* in 1995 by
Inter Varsity Press, Nottingham, England

Printed and bound by
Cox & Wyman, Ltd. Reading, Berkshire

Set in Garamond

Cover Design by Alister MacInnes

Contents

Introduction   7

PART ONE: EXPECTING THE KINGDOM
    1. Tumbling Kingdoms   11
    2. The Child Who Breaks Bars   25
    3. Whom The Mantle Fits   35

PART TWO: UNDERSTANDING THE KINGDOM
    4. They're Saying There's Another King   51
    5. Seven False Views   59
    6. The Enigma Of The Kingdom   73

PART THREE: HERALDING THE KINGDOM
    7. It's All About The Centre   85
    8. The Defeat Of Evil   95
    9. A Question Of Arithmetic   109

PART FOUR: LIVING THE KINGDOM
    10. The World Is Waiting For You   125
    11. Out In The Arena   137
    12. The Glory Of The Kingdom   151

Study Guide for Groups   165

Introduction

'So what's your alternative?' I asked my critic.

There were some thirty of us in the room, sipping drinks at a social get-together. I was coming under fire for my Christian beliefs, but now felt it was time to turn the tables on my inquisitor.

'Go on,' I pursued, 'describe to me your own world view.'

'World view? I haven't got one.'

'Oh, come!' I remonstrated. 'Every man, woman and child on the planet has a world view. Everyone has something to say about life and its meaning. So what do you believe?'

'Well, I'm an atheist.'

'No, no.' I couldn't let him go that easily. 'I'm not asking you what you *don't* believe. I'm asking you what you *do* believe.'

It was at this point that my acquaintance began to sound extremely unsure of himself. And yet I had only asked a couple of questions.

Developing a world view that is credible and will stand up against pressure and adversity isn't a particularly intellectual exercise, suited only to an academic élite. Suffering Christians in the Southern Sudan, devoid of Western schooling, gave the lie to that fallacy many decades ago. Their buoyant faith, anchored in the sovereign actions of God in history, emerged impregnable against an opposing world view that they resisted as inferior to their own – many of them to the point of death.

This book is written with the practical aim in mind of helping to equip the reader with a workable framework for all of life. What are the great landmarks that can give us a bearing in the complexities of living? How are we to stand up against – and to overthrow – the alien philosophies and movements that rampage our world today?

I repeat; we are not about to plod our way through a heavy piece of erudition. Nor will we engage in an exhaustive study of the kingdom of God.

We must leave that to the scholars. Instead, we shall go straight for the main compass points that enabled God's heroes and heroines of old to steer an unwavering course through the heavy seas of oppressive kingdoms and systems that claimed they were It.

What is the kingdom of God? Where shall we begin? Well... we could start back in the Garden of Eden. But let's not do that. We can learn instead from Homer, the epic Greek poet of the eighth century BC – who would begin at the great Moment, and let people pick up the story from there.

For me, the great moment, the vision of initial, overwhelming clarity, comes with the Old Testament prophet Daniel. Let's get started.

Richard Bewes
Written from All Souls Church,
Langham Place, London

Part One

Expecting the Kingdom

We need to realise that you cannot rightly understand God's ways at any point till you see them in the light of his sovereignty.

(James Packer, *I Want to be a Christian*, Kingsway)

1

Tumbling Kingdoms

A rock was cut out, but not by human hands. It struck the statue on its feet of iron and clay and smashed them. Then the iron, the clay, the bronze, the silver and the gold were broken to pieces at the same time and became like chaff on a threshing-floor in the summer. The wind swept them away without leaving a trace. But the rock that struck the statue became a huge mountain and filled the whole earth. (Daniel 2:34-35)

One day, late in June, in the year 168 BC, there took place one of the famous meetings of history, outside the city of Alexandria. A Roman and a Greek stood facing each other in direct confrontation.

The Greek – he was known as Antiochus Epiphanes – was marching with his army in a bid to grab Egypt and add it to his kingdom. His tyrannical rule was creating at that time the darkest period in all of Jewish history. But the power of Rome was beginning to be felt on the world stage. The Romans had fought and beaten Perseus of Macedon a few weeks earlier, and felt that they were just strong enough

11

to stop Antiochus. They sent a single senator, Lucius Popillius Laenas, to intercept him.

The two men met in the open countryside.

'The Roman Senate,' announced Popillius, 'desires that you withdraw your troops immediately, and return home.'

'I'll think about it,' promised Antiochus.

'No!' said Popillius – and with a stick he drew a circle in the sand round the feet of Antiochus Epiphanes. 'Answer me!' he challenged, 'before you get out of *that*!'

Antiochus complied, bowing before the incoming authority of a kingdom that was greater than his own, and quietly took his troops home. The day of the Greek was over, and it was done with a walking-stick.

The end for the Romans came over 500 years later, and it all happened on a single day, 24 August AD 410. Alaric, leader of the Visigoth hordes, accomplished the shocking impossibility of the sack of Rome, and Europe felt the reverberations for generations to come.

But I'm moving ahead too quickly; let's go back to the point – centuries earlier – when God's man, Daniel, foresaw in a golden, luminous moment of revelation the successive collapse of the kingdoms of this world, as against the steady growth of an alternative kingdom that will never be eclipsed.

Daniel, the young Hebrew – together with three of his companions – had been taken captive in 605BC, in the first of three deportations from Jerusalem, by

Nebuchadnezzar of Babylon. It is the home of modern Iraq.

Readers of the Bible are familiar with the story of the attempt by Nebuchadnezzar of a form of 'ethnic cleansing', as a selection of choice Hebrews was introduced to the ways of the Babylonian court; of the Famous Four's rejection of Nebuchadnezzar's menus in favour of a fibre diet; of their survival amid the intrigues that surrounded them; of the burning fiery furnace and the den of lions.

But it was Daniel's interpretation of Nebuchadnezzar's dream that caused the young man's rapid advance in the alien Babylonian kingdom. The details are given us in Daniel chapter 2, a linchpin passage for our understanding of God's rule in history.

Nebuchadnezzar had dreamed of a gigantic image, composed of four metals; the head of gold, torso and arms of silver, its trunk and thighs of bronze, and legs and feet of both iron and clay. This imposing statue was shattered into pieces by an incoming, hurtling rock, cut by no human hand – the stone growing eventually into a mountain that filled the whole earth.

'And you, O King Nebuchadnezzar,' pronounced the inspired prophet, 'you are the head of gold.' This is your moment! It's Babylon's turn. But all too soon three other great kingdoms would follow. The identity of the second and third kingdoms is given in Daniel 8:20-21, as being Medo-Persia and Greece.

It is only Rome that is not identified by name, as the fourth kingdom.

And the stone that became a mountain? Why, it is a kingdom set up by God and it will never be destroyed. It will preside over the downfall of every kingdom in sight and it will last for ever (Daniel 2:44-45).

It is this confidence that puts the cutting edge into the believer's communication and witness.

I recall speaking by interpretation in Moscow, not long after the old Soviet Union had ceased to exist. My interpreter was a young and very articulate Russian intellectual. I was to meet him again at Billy Graham's great Amsterdam Evangelism Congress in August 2000.

'I expect you grew up in a Christian family,' I hazarded.

'No, no,' replied Oleg. 'Five years ago I was an ardent member of the Communist Youth League and a committed atheist. I was a schoolteacher, and one day my headmaster sent for me. "There's trouble in the school," I was told. "A young girl is going around saying that she's a Christian. Worse than that – she's a Baptist! We can't have any of that. Go and shut her up, will you?"

'When I got to her,' continued Oleg, 'I got the surprise of my life. She was aged seven! But it got worse. As I began to remonstrate with her, her first question undermined me. "How sure are you that there is no God?"

'Inwardly I wasn't a 100 per cent certain and she sensed this. From that moment on she opened up my defences and led me to a faith in Jesus Christ that very day.'

'It was', admitted Oleg, 'the most humiliating moment of my entire life!'

It is a world view which has the Bible as its framework that explains such remarkable turn-arounds.

The young prophet Daniel's God-given perceptions gave him a similar advantage over Nebuchadnezzar's entire court of philosophers, for he could see the fragility of kingdoms such as Babylon's from a superior and eternal perspective. Four great kingdoms! But all of them were doomed. We know their dates well enough:

The Babylonian kingdom 605-539 BC
The Medo-Persian kingdom 539-331 BC
The Greek kingdom 331-63 BC
The Roman kingdom 63 BC-AD 410

Their overthrow was usually very quick. Babylon went in a single night, only forewarned by the divine 'writing on the wall' recorded in Daniel chapter 5. Nothing was going to survive the rock, cut by no human hand, that represented the unstoppable purposes of God in human affairs. Once you catch the vision of the rock that becomes a mountain and fills the whole earth, and – like Daniel – you've grasped the first of three massive ideas that colour all of life.

The shape of history

In some eastern faiths, history is a meaningless blank, for life on this world is understood as a never-ending, circular process. To ask where history is moving towards is a non-question. But Western-style materialism can also strip an individual of all sense of direction, reducing life to a 'cycle' of sleep, rise, eat, work, eat, work, watch TV, sleep, rise and eat.

The old hard-line Marxism was always doomed to disillusionment in its quest for a kind of utopian ideal, attainable on earth, towards which the human struggle was directed. Such a system can only end in the ashes of broken kingdoms everywhere.

Two thousand six hundred years ago, Daniel presented the world, through his interpretation of Nebuchadnezzar's dream, with a priceless key to the unlocking of the ages. History *does* have a shape and purpose. Follow the destiny of that stone and you'll find out!

As we read on in the book of Daniel, the picture becomes clearer still. By the time we reach the seventh chapter, fifty years have passed in the prophet's life. The dramatic seventh chapter! It records for us another 'dream', this time one of Daniel's own.

> Daniel said: 'In my vision at night I looked, and there before me were the four winds of heaven churning up the great sea. Four great beasts, each different from the others, came up out of the sea'.
>
> (Daniel 7:2-3)

In Bible understanding, 'the sea' always represents the ceaseless turbulence of human life in this world, the rise and fall of struggling nations (Isaiah 17:12; Revelation 17:15). Now, emerging out of the restless sea, Daniel dreams of four horrific freaks that represent – as in the earlier dream of the metallic statue – successive great empires unleashed upon the world.

Four great kingdoms. But, the argument could run, why concentrate on *them*?

Why, for example, no mention of the great dynasties in China, or South America? And why just the four?

Think it out for a moment. See if you can get there ahead of me. What we are presented with in the Scriptures is not simply the bare chronology of arid events and regimes. It is not history as such that we are confronted with in the Bible, but interpreted history; history viewed through God's binoculars. Now have you got there?

The reason that these four great empires feature in Daniel's vision is that we're looking at history as it affects the fortunes of God's people (the Jews in the Old Testament and the Christian church in the New). We are also looking at these developments as they represent the birth-pangs that preceded the coming of Jesus Christ, ruler of the kingdom that will outlast all others.

So it is a salvation-coloured panorama that the book of Daniel unfolds for us. Its kingdom-shaped history began to assume a global and universal

17

significance in the saving events of Christ's life and death at the time of the all-conquering fourth (the Roman) kingdom.

What of 'the little horn' that features in more than one instance (Daniel 7:8; 8:9)? This seems to be a kind of human incarnation of evil that surfaces periodically in history in order to usurp the place of God and to oppose his people. Daniel 8:9 seems to identify the terrible figure of Antiochus Epiphanes. This Greek tyrant, in 167 BC, was to claim divinity for himself, desecrate the Jewish temple, and ban all observance of the Jewish law.

Many 'antichrist' figures have arisen, and will culminate towards the end of time in a final and ultimate 'man of lawlessness' (2 Thessalonians 2:3-4), who will be overthrown by Jesus Christ at his return. Believers are not to be obsessed with identifying who this figure is, for all our energies could be taken up on such an activity. Rather we are to be absorbed with Christ himself, who has no beginning or end.

This is the point of the second and third chapters of Daniel. Here is the very shape of history – that the various successive world powers have no permanence. In contrast, there will grow 'an ever-lasting dominion that will not pass away' (Daniel 7:14).

The book of Daniel's portrayal of the shape of history introduces the second great concept of these chapters.

The rule of God

Stay in Daniel 7, and see the dramatic scene switch!
No hurtling rock, as in chapter 2. Now we are
looking at a person – and a throne.

> As I looked, thrones were set in place,
> and the Ancient of Days took his seat.
> His clothing was as white as snow;
> the hair of his head was white like wool.
> His throne was flaming with fire,
> and its wheels were all ablaze (Daniel 7:9).

There are thrones in this scene, but only one of
them has any significance, and it is the only one
permanently occupied. Gone is the disorder of the
freakish beasts and the disturbed sea; now all is
controlled, and brilliantly majestic.

Daniel is looking at heaven itself, and the centre
of all rule. The prophet Ezekiel saw something very
similar in chapter 1 of his prophecy. At the end of
the Bible, we discover that the apostle John witnessed
a similar scene in the fourth chapter of the book of
Revelation, in his vision of God's throne, surrounded
by its myriads of angelic attendants and singers. It is
this throne, emphasize these Bible writers, that is the
centre of all rule. If the centre is intact, then nothing
else matters – however great the propaganda and
violence emitted from the kingdoms of earth. They
may be allowed to operate for a limited period of
time (Daniel 7:12), but they exercise no overall
control.

Whether it was the third-century emperor Diocletian, – who even had a medal struck to commemorate the demise of the Christian faith – or the twenty-first century Muslim leaders in Indonesia, our opponents have never grasped that the sure-fire way of strengthening the work of Christ is to pressurize it. I recall the terror of the Idi Amin regime in Uganda, during the 1970s. One of the Christian leaders there said later on BBC radio, 'Amin seemed immovable. He was as solid as a mountain. Then some of us remembered that if you have faith as small as a mustard seed, even mountains can be moved!' And so it proved to be.

A third door into our understanding is opened by these chapters of Daniel.

The coming of Christ

How we tingle with expectation when we hear that a great one is on the way! It may be a famous singer or a sports personality. When I was a teenager I went with my brother and a friend to see the mighty Australian tennis player, Frank Sedgman. We got to the tennis stadium so early that only the chief groundsman was ahead of us. All morning we waited by the courtside. Just to see the man! Then at 2 pm, as Sedgman walked down the steps and on to court, we feasted our gaze on him – that is, until his eye fell on me! It was too much: at that point I had to look away.

When it comes to the pivotal person of history, the vibrations about his coming were felt centuries ahead. Here is Daniel in his own description of the coming world leader:

> In my vision at night I looked, and there before me was one like a son of man, coming with the clouds of heaven. He approached the Ancient of Days and was led into his presence. He was given authority, glory and sovereign power; all peoples, nations and men of every language worshipped him. His dominion is an everlasting dominion that will not pass away, and his kingdom is one that will never be destroyed. (Daniel 7:13-14)

Of course, we wonder what 'a son of man' was doing in heaven. The answer is that here, evidently, is Representative Man, standing universally on behalf of the whole human race. He comes with the clouds which, biblically, are associated with the activity of God and with his covenant.

And then is he human or is he God? He is certainly not an angel, for angels have earlier been listed among those surrounding the throne. He can only be divine, being worthy of universal worship. 'Son of Man' – it was Jesus Christ's favourite self-designation. Although the title pointed to his messianic divinity, it didn't carry the particular political connotation of leadership that he was always careful to avoid.

Certainly the Jewish people recognized the divinity of the figure in Daniel's dream. When Jesus said to his accusers in Matthew 26:64, 'In the future you will see the Son of Man sitting at the right hand of the Mighty One and coming on the clouds of heaven,'

he was applying the figure of Daniel's vision directly
to himself, and so invited the charge of blasphemy
from the high priest.

Christ is seen in these flashes of glory throughout
the history of God's people. He appears on the
Mount of Transfiguration, irradiated and dazzling.
Stephen the martyr sees him in glory shortly before
his death, and quotes from Daniel, 'I see heaven open
and the Son of Man standing at the right hand of
God' (Acts 7:56). The apostle John in his exile on
the island of Patmos collapses at the vision of
'someone "like a son of man" – His head and hair
were white like wool, as white as snow, and his eyes
were like blazing fire' (Revelation 1:13-14). The
descriptive language is similar in each instance, and
Daniel 2 and 7 are the fundamental, epic chapters.

And by way of a postscript, we needn't be too
anxious about the old liberal Bible critics who insisted
that the author of Daniel's prophecy must have been
a later writer; that the real Daniel couldn't have
predicted ahead of his time the behaviour of
Antiochus Epiphanes or the identity of future
kingdoms. Why, they maintain, this later author was
in fact hopelessly inaccurate with the details of
Daniel's own period. There's no record, say these
critics, of 'Belshazzar' ever having been on the
Babylonian throne – a contemporary writer would
have known that Nabonidus was the king at that
time. The author of Daniel, they insist, was not Daniel
but some anonymous Jew who lived three centuries
later.

What those critics didn't know was what archaeology subsequently confirmed – that Belshazzar was made co-regent of the country by his father Nabonidus in 556 BC, while Nabonidus was away, campaigning in central Arabia; this we learn from the Nabonidus Chronicle.

Little evidences of a first-hand acquaintance with current events slip out in Daniel's writings. When, for example, Belshazzar promises that if the prophet can interpret his dream, he'll make him 'the third highest ruler in the kingdom' (Daniel 5:16), it makes perfect sense. He couldn't have offered him the second place, because it was he who was the second ruler!

It is probably the same with 'Darius the Mede' who took over the Babylonian kingdom (Daniel 5:31). Surely, it is claimed, it was *Cyrus* who headed up the incoming Medo-Persian empire? The likelihood, however, is that they reigned together; certainly they are named together (Daniel 6:28). It seems clear that this Darius was different from the one who came after Cyrus.

What a vision was Daniel's! If his world-view gave him and his three companions in captivity an understanding of history and its shape, of the rule of God and of the coming of Christ, it is small wonder that they could defy the very worst that Nebuchadnezzar could do. His kingdom was tumbling. They embraced a different world-view. The kingdom they served was a rock that would clear a path for them and their spiritual descendants throughout the annals of our human story.

It is when we move back another hundred years in Old Testament prophecy, and look at the Identikit of the coming world ruler, that we find we are in for a surprise.

2

The Child Who Breaks Bars

The people walking in darkness
    have seen a great light...
For as in the day of Midian's defeat,
    you have shattered
the yoke that burdens them,
    the bar across their shoulders,
    the rod of their oppressor.
For to us a child is born,
    to us a son is given,
    and the government will be on his shoulders.
And he will be called
    Wonderful Counsellor, Mighty God,
    Everlasting Father, Prince of Peace.
Of the increase of his government and peace
    there will be no end.

                                    (Isaiah 9:2, 4, 6-7)

The following story emerged at the great
'Lausanne II' Congress on World Evangelization at
Manila in 1989.

In a prison camp for dissidents, run by one of
the world's notorious totalitarian regimes, a saintly
pastor was singled out for the lowest punishment

of all – working in the sewer pit, into which all the prison's sanitary waste flowed. The prisoner was required to wade out into the two-metre pool and keep the mass of filth moving onward on its journey.

This the pastor regularly did without protest. When he had waded to the middle he would begin to sing at the top of his voice. No warders intervened; indeed no-one dared approach him. As he later told the delegates at Manila, a favourite song that he would sing as a witness to others and as fellowship with his Lord ran as follows:

> I come to the garden alone,
> While the dew is still on the roses,
> And the voice I hear, falling on my ear,
> The Son of God discloses:
>
> And He walks with me and He talks with me,
> And He tells me I am His own.
> And the joy we share as we tarry there,
> None other has ever known.

It is hardly surprising that by the end of the story, many of the congress delegates were broken down in weeping.

But such inspiring accounts of faith that overcomes have been repeated throughout history; of men and women 'who through faith conquered kingdoms' (Hebrews 11:33). But how do you conquer kingdoms of the stature of Pharaoh's, Nebuchadnezzar's or Caesar's?

'A Child provides the explanation,' declared the prophet Isaiah in a passage that inspired the writing of Handel's Messiah. Under the ministry that he would exercise, heavy yokes would give way and solid bars would shatter! He would emerge as the great Illuminator of people walking in darkness. He would be renowned as the great Comforter. Many would look to him as the great Liberator, and he would triumph as the divine and mighty Governor.

There are, in all, four great characteristics of his kingdom:

- Peace
- Righteousness
- Universality
- Permanence

From the start of the Bible we become aware of God's kingdom and its development from small beginnings. God establishes his contract with Abraham, the prototype believer, that he is to be a father of many nations (Genesis 17:4-7).

Michael Lawson, a Jewish Christian believer, writes:

What a vision. To India, Russia, Spain, Great Britain, the United States, Ethiopia, Jubuti, Italy and New Zealand, in fact to anywhere where there are true believers in this same God – the God of Abraham, the God and Father of Jesus Christ – this universal promise to Abraham is extended (*The Unfolding Kingdom*, Christian Focus).

And the vision holds, despite the failure of Abraham's descendants, the nation of Israel, to exhibit the qualities of God's rule to the surrounding nations. God's laws are defied, his prophets rejected, his rule compromised. By the time Isaiah presented his prophecy, around 733 BC, the nation of Israel has split into two, and the twilight is closing in on the southern kingdom of Judah, with the rise of Assyria under its leader Tiglath Pileser – the biggest armed menace that the world had ever seen.

And yet, 'Your God reigns' (Isaiah 52:7).

A royal Child, a wonder-Child, was coming! Isaiah, writing as he did 700 years ahead of the birth at Bethlehem, displayed a 'telescopic' view of the future, like so many of his contemporaries. Events both far and near merge together as description follows description. When would people experience the blessings of such a future kingdom? And how complete would be the fulfilment?

Here is a quote from a theologian, the late Ernest Kevan:

> The fulfilment of biblical prophecy always transcends the categories in which the prophecy was first given.

A prophet of the eighth century BC would speak in the context of an immediate impending crisis, and of the need of physical deliverance from military oppression. But under the inspiration of God, the utterance was also intended to reverberate far beyond – to horizons and spiritual dimensions that will affect millions of people world-wide.

There is what we could call, first of all, the local and partial fulfilment of a prophecy; secondly, there is the gospel and spiritual fulfilment at the time of Christ's ministry. But we can take it further still and recognize that the prophecy will have a final and eternal fulfilment at the end of time as we know it, when the kingdom of God sees its ultimate completion.

So certain was Isaiah of the fulfilment of his prophecy that he writes in what we may call 'the tense of the prophetic past' – as though the event has already taken place!

The people walking in darkness
  have seen a great light (Isaiah 9:2).

It is this confidence in the superiority of God's greater and permanent kingdom that keeps its members buoyant even in the heaviest of oppressive seas.

This was Moses' secret, centuries ahead of Isaiah. In one of the great speeches of history he bids his dying farewell to the people of Israel, warns them, and refers to the alien life-styles and philosophies with which they were surrounded – denouncing them as being inferior – even on the admission of their critics!

> For their rock is not like our Rock,
> as even our enemies concede (Deuteronomy 32:31).

Israel's neighbours knew that they had nothing that could compete with the Rock of monotheism, the Rock of the ten commandments, the Rock of the divine covenant, or the Rock of spiritual worship.

Moses embraced this conviction, and so did the apostle Paul in New Testament times. In their own turn, Augustine, Dante, Calvin and Dostoevsky restated it. Could there ever be a foundation for belief and living that can compare with the Rock that carried Moses; that in gospel times caused Christianity's critics to complain of 'these who have turned the world upside down'?

Like Moses, the early Christians knew how to challenge hostile kingdoms and to defy the thought-systems of an entire continent. They would die, rather than compromise with the multi-faith set-up of Rome's Pantheon. They would not permit Jesus to share an honoured position alongside other 'deities', for he was Lord alone. Later, when the emperor Domitian proclaimed himself *Dominus et Deus* ('Lord and God'), a further collision was inevitable.

Liberal theologians in Western society today speak of Christians who believe in the uniqueness of Jesus and his kingdom as an anachronism; of the need to come to terms with today's plurality of faiths and to

accommodate these other beliefs – as though such a
situation has never presented itself before! They
evidently have forgotten the infinitely more diverse
religious scene that confronted the early apostolic
preaching of the Christian faith.

The Assyrians thought that their culture would
rule supreme over that of Israel. Isaiah thought
differently. Is it just an accident that Christ's name,
on all five continents, is a more familiar word than
Ashur, Hamath, or Arpad? What was it in Christ
and his kingdom that beat down all memory of
these names that once ruled supreme? Serapis,
Mithras, Osiris and Jupiter were all obliterated in
turn.

In recent years we have seen the rise of the New
Age movement. Business executives in some of the
world's great cities have been told that they were
god – that, this being so, there was nothing that they
could not achieve. How long can be the life-span of
such a movement? It doesn't take all that long for
enthusiastic devotees to discover that the dream has
faded, that they are transparently not god-like beings;
that they have problems with their colleagues, their
deadlines, their marriages.

It is with humility, but also confidence, that across
the ages another conviction has voiced itself: 'Their
rock is not like our Rock.' We've only to make a few
comparisons for the point to register!

Whose life was the more securely based: that of
Moses, a foundational leader of civilizations, or
Pharaoh, the all-powerful world ruler of his time?

Who had the moral superiority between Daniel, the visionary of the world's kingdoms, and the military genius Nebuchadnezzar? Put the desert-living John the Baptist up against the paranoid Herod who had him beheaded – whose integrity would we trust? Or Mary who sat at Jesus' feet in Bethany, compared with Salome the dancing girl? Salome might have made the tabloid front pages, but we'd have trusted Mary with anything that required moral responsibility.

We could go on – Paul the pioneering apostle and his captor, Felix, the Roman governor who paled before Paul's preaching; Archbishop Janani Luwum in our modern times, and his opposite number in Uganda, the towering Idi (President for Life) Amin who killed his critic with two shots, in a fit of rage. Those two shots say it all. Amin couldn't take the pressure from his moral superior.

The test comes when life turns difficult; when the tides of bereavement are swirling around you, when the spectre of job shortages taps you on the shoulder, when the headlines day after day are bleak, when daily circumstances insist, 'There's no meaning to life.'

Take Voltaire, that bitter eighteenth-century critic of the church. It was when he was on his deathbed that he sent for the clergyman. His last letter, dated 2 March 1778, ended:

> I did confess to him that if it please God to dispose of me, I would die in the church in which I was born. Hoping that the Divine mercy will pardon

my faults, I sign myself in the presence of Abbé
Mignon my nephew, and Marquis de Villeville my
friend,

VOLTAIRE.

At the crisis moments the issue presents itself: how
does the framework on which you have built your
life measure up as a credible kingdom to have
invested in?

- How stable is it?
- How dependable is it?
- How durable is it?
- How accessible is it – can I come to it and
  find satisfying answers?

These questions matter acutely when the Assyrians
or Babylonians are on the border. Is God in control?
Is he our king? Does he rule all nations?

Yes! declared Abraham and the patriarchs. Yes!
sang Moses as he concluded his song by the Red Sea
with the words, 'The Lord will reign for ever and
ever' (Exodus 15:18). Yes! wrote the psalmist as he
caught a preview of the universal messianic kingdom
in these words:

'Ask of me, and I will make the nations your
inheritance, the ends of the earth your possession.
You will rule them with an iron sceptre; you will
dash them to pieces like pottery.' (Psalm 2:8-9)

Yes! said Daniel's three companions as they stood on the edge of Nebuchadnezzar's furnace.

'If we are thrown into the blazing furnace, the God we serve is able to save us from it, and he will rescue us from your hand, O king. But even if he does not, we want you to know, O king, that we will not serve your gods or worship the image of gold you have set up'.   (Daniel 3:17-18)

Which was blazing the hottest – Nebuchadnezzar's furnace, or the defiant conviction that God's sovereign purposes controlled everything, whether or not death was imminent?

To adapt a sentiment of the late Malcolm Muggeridge: I'd rather be wrong with Daniel and his friends, with Elijah, Isaiah, John the Baptist, Mary or Paul – I'd rather be wrong, in such a company, than be right with Nebuchadnezzar, Jezebel, Tiglath Pileser of Assyria, Herod, Salome or Felix, let alone Voltaire, the Huxleys, H. G. Wells or Bertrand Russell!

But the birth of the Child himself gives us the clearest signal yet that *we aren't in the wrong kingdom*. Let us turn to the event that splits the dispensations BC and AD.

3

Whom The Mantle Fits

Then I saw in the right hand of him who sat on the throne a scroll with writing on both sides and sealed with seven seals. And I saw a mighty angel proclaiming in a loud voice, 'Who is worthy to break the seals and open the scroll?' But no-one in heaven or on earth or under the earth could open the scroll or even look inside it. I wept and wept because no-one was found who was worthy to open the scroll or look inside. (Revelation 5:1-4)

Like the rare edelweiss of the Swiss mountain-sides, true leadership is an elusive phenomenon. It takes more than oratorical brilliance or organizational genius to bring it into play. The capacity to inspire others lies close to its heart. The men who fought in the army of Alexander the Great found in their leader a man who shared their rations, their anxieties and their reverses to such a degree that they could follow him anywhere.

Listen to him at Opis in Mesopotamia, as he addresses his troops:

'I have no part of my body, in front at least, that is left without scars; there is no weapon, used at close quarters, or hurled from afar, of which I do not carry the mark. I have been wounded by the sword, shot with arrows, struck from a catapult, smitten many times with stones and clubs – for you, for your glory, for your wealth.'

The ceaseless quest of the human spirit, however, has been for a leader who can command such universal allegiance as to rise above the title of 'The Great' and gain recognition as 'The Only'. Such is the theme of the famous fifth chapter of the book of Revelation.

In his lonely exile on the island of Patmos, the apostle John sees 'heaven opened' in a series of visions that depict the irresistible triumph of the kingdom of God. The brilliant imagery of the heavenly throne in chapter 4, however, gives place in the next chapter to a different scene where an agonizing search is portrayed.

It is not unlike the fable of Cinderella, in which a nation-wide appeal is made for the individual whose foot will fit the delicate glass slipper discarded by the untraceable princess. Only when the slipper fits can the true aspirant for the prince's hand be recognized and acclaimed!

But Revelation presents us with no fable. The dilemma was real enough to God's apostle. The central figure on the divine throne holds a scroll in his hand, sealed with seven seals. The angelic challenge is made universally ('in a loud voice', Revelation 5:2): 'Who is worthy to break the seals and open the scroll?'

The key word is 'worthy'. It occurs four times in the chapter. Here is the scroll containing the secrets, the destiny and the meaning of our world and of all existence. But is there anyone 'worthy' enough to be found who can break the seals and decipher the scroll's contents satisfactorily and for all time?

No harder task

The vision of Revelation 5 expresses perfectly the longing of the ages. Is there anyone who can give us a credible explanation of life, of its direction and goal? What is the sense in the humdrum events that make up the average day of one of earth's citizens? What is the whole thing for?

No harder task could possibly be set. It is more than the unravelling of the mystery of life. For in the breaking of the seals there seems to be implied the additional task of actioning the divine programme for the ages. It is not enough for the aspiring candidate simply to be a commentator and interpreter. On top there is a further colossal requirement – to be the executive of the programme, and carry it through!

The contention of the Christian faith is that the search ends with the figure of Jesus. We note how the Roman empire, at the apex of its power, unwittingly opened the door to the fulfilment of an ancient prophecy – that the coming world leader would be born at Bethlehem:

But you, Bethlehem Ephrathah,
    though you are small among the clans of Judah,
out of you will come for me
    one who will be ruler over Israel,
whose origins are from of old,
    from ancient times (Micah 5:2).

The greatness of this figure would 'reach to the ends of the earth' (Micah 5:4).

Humanly speaking, Bethlehem could not possibly have been the birthplace of Jesus, but for the passion for organization that so characterized the Romans. In particular, Caesar Augustus, in his fifty-seven-year rule, transformed Rome from a republic into an empire, and – as he boasted – 'found the city built of brick and left it built of marble'. For Augustus, control was everything; nothing must be left to chance. All was to be organized, annotated, registered! And so every several years a census would be announced.

The obsession for organization required the cumbersome arrangement that all citizens register at their town of origin – and we can imagine Joseph and Mary groaning at the thought of making the eighty mile journey to Joseph's ancestral City of David, Bethlehem. Preparations for the impending birth would already have been made at their home in Nazareth. Joseph, as a craftsman, would have seen to it that a cot was ready.

And then, suddenly – Augustus and his craze for a census! The mother-to-be might have been excused for wondering whether she and her future baby were nothing but pawns in a vast game of historical chess over which she had no control.

Had Augustus known it, had the census-organizer Quirinius known it – they were the pawns, not in a game, but in a divine and benevolent plan bigger than history itself. It was out of the hands of Mary and Joseph; the details for the fulfilling of the prophecy were taken care of, courtesy of the world's most powerful man. The divine message was, 'If I require it, I can make all the ramifications of a mighty kingdom work for this one event.'

But could the Bethlehem baby be the authentic leader of an eternal kingdom and the Interpreter of all the ages? Here was the child of an unknown peasant woman, brought up in a village so insignificant as to receive no mention in the Old Testament. Could his influence even dent the Roman empire, let alone stretch beyond to India, Japan, America, Iceland? 'Who is worthy to open the scroll?' The challenge is flung before the whole world!

There is no harder task, and John the visionary becomes overwhelmed at the magnitude of it.

No sadder cry

No-one, it seems, in all creation, is able to open the scroll or to gain even a peep at its contents. 'I wept and wept,' declares the apostle (Revelation 5:4).

Of course. To miss the plot, even at the level of a detective novel or a television play is frustrating enough. I remember being taken to see Tom

Stoppard's play *Hapgood*. Having been warned by my American host that the play was difficult to follow, I was on the edge of my seat as the curtain went up. It was to no avail; within the first minute I had lost the thread irretrievably. My only comfort came on leaving the theatre and seeing the quote from a newspaper review on the advertisement hoarding outside: 'You don't have to be Einstein to understand this play, but it helps.'

It is no help, however, to be Einstein, Plato or Aristotle when it comes to cracking the cipher of our own existence. The Greek tragedian Euripides wrote plays such as *Medea* that can be seen today – but his observation from the fifth century BC could have been written for our own time:

> As I look on the chances that fall to men and the deeds they do, it is confusion, all of it, and life passes away for men, full of wandering and change for ever.

A century earlier Xenophanes wrote: 'Guesswork is over all.'

On this count it is of no particular advantage to have been born in the twentieth century. Clever and prominent individuals find themselves similarly frustrated. The diaries of a well-known British entertainer were published after his death. One August day he had written:

I wonder if anyone will ever know about the emptiness of my life? I wonder if anyone will ever stand in a room that I have lived in, and touch the things that were once a part of my life, and wonder about me, and ask themselves what manner of man I was. How to ever tell them? How to ever explain?

His last entry of all read, 'O what's the bloody point?' (*The Kenneth Williams Diaries*, Harper Collins).

It is not that the world has been short of contenders for the title role of Interpreter of life for the human race. There have been many. Individuals have arisen, meteor-like, into the skies of philosophical and religious speculation. Whole movements and systems of thought have prevailed for considerable periods of time. Region after region around the world has put forward an aspirant for the post of Universal Teacher.

Whether it was the animism of ancient civilizations, the lure of the East, or the dialectical materialism of Karl Marx, each showed us something of wisdom and understanding, but so often there has been an accompanying wistfulness.

Into our own church of All Souls in central London, an Iraqi came one day. He was a dedicated Communist and his name was Ivan Fawzi. By a friend he was introduced to our outreach course *Christianity Explored*. Week after week he brought his arguments to bear upon the course leader, my colleague Rico Tice. 'I fought him every inch,' declared Ivan. But in Ivan's life there was an underlying wistfulness and a

disillusionment with Communism. The day was to
come when the magnetism of Christ won over the
young Iraqi. He was to become a fearless open air
preacher in London, and a participant, not only in
Christianity Explored, but also in our follow-up
international video teaching course, *Open Home, Open
Bible.*

In making the great decision to follow Christ so
many of us, in varying ways, have come to the end
of a protracted search, turning reluctantly away from
alternative claimants upon our loyalty: 'you had a lot
to offer me but you're not the one.'

The evangelist John, then, as he weeps at the
inability of the entire cosmos to produce an adequate
inspirer for the human race, only expresses an age-
old despair. There is no sadder cry. The incarnation,
however, changes everything.

No fitter candidate

In his vision, one of twenty-four elders comforts
John:

> 'Do not weep! See, the Lion of the tribe of Judah,
> the Root of David, has triumphed. He is able to
> open the scroll and its seven seals.' Then I saw a
> Lamb, looking as if it had been slain, standing in
> the centre of the throne... He came and took the
> scroll from the right hand of him who sat on the
> throne (Rev. 5:5-7).

The Lion of Judah and the Root of David –
here are two royal titles that designate the figure who
now takes centre stage. We crane our necks to catch
a glimpse of this kingly personage! What more
powerful image than a lion? Then comes the surprise.

Earthly kingdoms have tended to adopt
impressive symbols – the American spread eagle,
the Russian bear, the British lion. Not so in this case.
The kingdom of God chooses for its symbol a Lamb,
a Lamb that has in fact been slain. It is this figure,
paradoxically, that breaks open the riddle of our
existence.

'Why should your God come and live on earth?'
asked the second-century pagan philosopher Celsus.
'Didn't he know what was going on there?'

The birth at Bethlehem, the death at Jerusalem
and the resurrection of Easter give the answer. The
simplest and the youngest could at last understand
that there is meaning, personality and a relationship
of love at the heart of our universe; that the Creator
of everything has troubled himself with our little
affairs, visiting, serving, suffering and dying.

It is the Lamb, insist the New Testament writers,
who provides the explanation and the goal of all of
our living. From Genesis to Revelation the answer
has been building up – the beginning and the end;
creation and the consummation of all things. The
shackles of rigid determinism melt away before its
onslaught. The negative message of a meaningless
universe shatters into pieces.

'Do not weep!' says the Scripture. The Lamb has done it all – a Lamb that has been slain, for, in John's vision, it is now all too obviously alive as it comes forward and takes the scroll of destiny and, to the acclaim of every onlooker, emerges as the perfect, qualified Interpreter the world had been waiting for. The kingdom of God is headed by a unique King. There is no fitter candidate. It is at this point in John's vision that the singing begins!

No sweeter music
Had Celsus lived a little later, he would have received the answer to his cynical question from the great classical fourth-century writer, Ephraem the Syrian. In moving terms he writes of Christ's coming:

Child of Bethlehem, what contrasts you embrace! No-one has ever been so humble; no-one has ever wielded such power. We stand in awe of your holiness, and yet we are bathed in your love.

And where shall we look for you? You are in high heaven, in the glory of the Godhead. Yet those who searched for you on earth found you in a tiny baby at Mary's breast. We come in hushed reverence to find you as God, and you welcome us as man. We come unthinkingly to find you as man, and are blinded by the light of your Godhead.

You are the heir to David's throne, but you renounced all of his royal splendour. Of all his luxurious bedrooms, you chose a stable. Of all his magnificent beds, you chose a feeding trough. Of all his golden chariots, you chose an ass.

Never was there a king like you! Instead of royal isolation, you made yourself available to everyone who needed you. Instead of high security, you made yourself vulnerable to those who hated you.

It is we who need you, above anything in the world. You give yourself to us with such total generosity, that it might almost seem that you need us.

There never was a king like this before!

But we are not short of modern tributes to the power of Christ to unlock our human puzzles. Hassan Dehqani-Tafti of Iran, a convert from Islam, has written in recent times:

It was the fact of the Incarnation which made me fall in love with Christianity. 'God was in Christ reconciling the world to himself' (2 Corinthians 5:19). To a Muslim the very idea of God becoming man is blasphemous, but it was this 'blasphemy' that saved me from unbelief. To me it came to be the most natural thing (*Design of my World*, Lutterworth Press).

The Incarnation – and all of its saving sequel – teaches us that the kingdom of God is tied right into the everyday activities and recreations of ordinary life. There are certain leaders of modern belief systems who never begin to reflect the sheer earthiness of the incarnation. They are too 'religious', if anything; stern, forbidding and unsmiling. It would be difficult to imagine them laughing at a joke, going

to a party (as Jesus did), or settling down to a game
of Scrabble.

By contrast, the members of God's new order
sing. Endlessly repeated *mantras* or chants are not for
us. The great hymns of the kingdom age roll down
the centuries, from the congregations who read Paul's
letters (e.g. Ephesians 5:14), right through Charles
Wesley and Isaac Watts, and on to our present-day
hymn-writers. And our hymns of joy are but
reflections of the 'new song' with which the vast
heavenly company of John's vision extol the Lamb:

> You are worthy to take the scroll
>   and to open its seals,
> because you were slain,
>   and with your blood you purchased men
>   for God
>   from every tribe and language
>   and people and nation.
> You have made them to be a kingdom and
>   priests to serve our God,
> and they will reign on the earth (Rev. 5:9-10).

The 'worthiness' of the New Testament Greek
indicates moral character. It is not a 'powerful' person
that we have been waiting for, so much as someone
of transparent goodness and trustworthiness. The
theme of the celestial singers in the Revelation is that
the waiting is over; that there is not a region or tribal
grouping anywhere that Christ the Lamb did not
die for in redeeming love.

John Stott rejects the idea that Jesus was one of many great spiritual leaders. He writes:

> It would be hopelessly incongruous to refer to him as 'Jesus the Great', comparable to Alexander the Great, Charles the Great or Napoleon the Great. Jesus is not 'the Great'; he is the only. He has no peers, no rivals and no successors (*The Contemporary Christian*, Inter-Varsity Press).

Truly the mantle fits. Here is the one leader with the capacity to form a world-wide kingdom – the Alpha and the Omega, the Lion of the tribe of Judah, the Root and Offspring of David, the Bright Morning Star, the Rider on the white horse who summons us to ride with him into our rocking, reeling world.

So we can sing:

Christ holds the keys of death and hell,
The First and Last, and Living One.
His rule proclaim, his triumph tell!
For through his Cross his work is done.

Though powers of darkness make their claim,
Though wars may rage and kingdoms fall,
The throne of Christ shall stay the same;
And all must heed his trumpet call.

Christ breaks the seal around the scroll,
Opens the meaning of our world.
He leads us forward to our goal,
The secrets of all life unfurled.

See death and famine riding by,
With war and sickness drawing near.
We'll ride with Christ until we die,
And wait his reign in glory here.
© R. T. Bewes, *Sing Glory*, 431, Jubilate Hymns

Part Two

Understanding the Kingdom

The reign of Jesus is real. Made fact by his death and resurrection, it is only recognized by His people. Jesus will end creation's history by His return and will demonstrate to all the world that He is indeed King in God's world. He will do that by judging us all.

(John C. Chapman, *A Fresh Start*, Hodder & Stoughton)

4

They're Saying There's Another King

'These men who have turned the world upside down have come here also and they are all acting against the decrees of Caesar, saying that there is another king, Jesus.'   (Acts 17:6-7, RSV)

It must have been around AD 50 when a stubby man, speaking in Greek with an eastern Mediterranean accent, stood on a shoulder of rock in Athens, addressing a group of sceptics. Nearby, towering above him, was the Acropolis, and high upon it stood the mighty Parthenon.

No backcloth for a speech on a new religion could have provided a worse start! The Parthenon was then nearly five centuries old, but the marble seemed as fresh and new as if it had just left the sculptor. It was the perfect symbol of permanence and universality, a monument to the prevailing religious and philosophical consensus that then ruled the minds of thinking people across Europe. Only

Jews and a few scattered groups such as Druids had a different mindset.

Now here was a Jew, advocating a completely different way of looking at life – and telling an unbelievable story! His listeners had only to shift their eyes by a few degrees, there on Mars' Hill, and glance at the Parthenon, to realize the absurdity of what they were hearing. And when Paul of Tarsus reached the point that the rule of the one true God would culminate in 'a day' when the whole world would be held to account by an appointed Man who had been raised from the dead, the laughter could no longer be held back, and the gathering began to break up. With a few exceptions, the citizens of Athens forgot Paul swiftly.

But it wasn't the last of Paul's message, as far as Athens was concerned.

By AD 435 or thereabouts, the Parthenon itself had been designated a Christian church – and a Christian church it remained for a thousand years.

In 1456 the Turks took Athens. In 1687 a Venetian shell, aimed by a German, crashed through the roof of the Parthenon. The powder stored there blew up and left the famous building very much as we see it today. The Turks were expelled in 1833, and no trace of them was left.

What a strange history! The Stoics and Epicureans, listening to Paul that day (Acts 17:16-34), would have been surprised in their laughter if they could have foreseen that the Christian faith would hold the Parthenon longer than the religion of the Greeks.

Not that the control of a mere building is of any ultimate importance. What was important was the power of a new thought-form to overturn the astounding mix of cultures and creeds that had been fused into a towering world religion.

How *could* one great system such as this be replaced? It was so adaptable as to embrace and absorb every philosophy in sight – Delphi with its Oracle, the rites of the Egyptian Isis, Cybele the Mother of Gods in Asia.

Romans could go to Greece and identify their own Jupiter with Zeus, or visit Syria and find him in Baal. The historian T. R. Glover writes of this as one of the most significant questions in all history – how could such an immense switch come about?

Four fundamental weaknesses in the old system give us the clue.

First, it failed to produce a satisfying interpretation of life. 'The unexamined life', Plato had said centuries earlier, 'is not livable for a human being.' By that he meant that every system of thought and outlook must be able to withstand a rigorous intellectual assault; you couldn't live for ever on the basis of a tradition. At some point the question will raise itself, 'Does life, as it has been explained to me by my upbringing, make any sense?' On this count, the hitherto all-pervading structures were vulnerable to the preachers of a new and different kingdom.

Secondly, the old forms failed to produce a credible morality. Such morality as there was came from the poets rather than the temples and the priests: the 'heroes' of Greek mythology demonstrated a higher morality than the gods themselves! The deepest human need – supremely that of forgiveness – could not be met.

Thirdly, those early thinkers were unable to offer a personal faith. The world was not short of deities, but polytheism consistently led its worshippers into a cul-de-sac of fear, not faith. At every turn there was a different god to be taken account of, propitiated, appeased! There was a kingdom of demons too, forever threatening and hostile. Here, by contrast, was a new message, proclaiming one God who had 'rescued us from the dominion of darkness and brought us into the kingdom of the Son he loves' (Colossians 1:13).

To the relief of the second-century Christian apologist Tatian, the 'tyranny of ten thousand gods' had been replaced by the loving monarchy of one.

Fourthly, the ancient world could not come up with an answer to death. Wise philosophers mumbled into their beards late through the night, struggling with the phantom of the grave. Incantations were prescribed, charms and rituals, feasts and observances – but the fear remained. Nobody had the faintest clue; none could shed even a chink of light on the grim topic. The epitaphs on old tombstones and in ancient literature highlight the despair, the cynicism and bitterness with which death was viewed everywhere:

> Child, be not overly distressed. I was not, I was born, I lived, I am not...that is all.

All we are kept for death, fed like a herd of swine
that are butchered, without rhyme or reason. (From
the Greek Anthology)

On all four fronts, where the old world failed,
the friends of Jesus succeeded. In the power of the
Spirit of Pentecost, they launched the message of
Christ's kingdom on a tidal wave of joy and creativity
that has touched the world of art, literature, music,
education, medicine, politics and law. It was, in fact,
a shockwave that up-ended virtually every
preconceived idea in sight.

There were running feet on the day that Jesus
was raised from death; slamming doors, breakdowns
in communication and exclamations of unbelief.
Swiftly the news spread: Someone – on behalf of
the whole human race – has done it, has beaten down
the most feared of all our enemies, including death
itself and life can never be the same again.

It was new. It was shocking. And it was
controversial. These were the people who 'turned
the world upside down, saying that there is another
King, Jesus'. Despite the hostility of the vested
interests and the religious prejudice, the indomitable
disciples stuck to their story.

This has been remarked on by Chuck Colson,
who is remembered as the 'hatchet man' in the
administration of former American president
Richard Nixon. Along with others, he was implicated
in the notorious Watergate scandal that rocked the

nation and brought down the President. In later days Colson – whose experiences of trial and prison led to his becoming a Christian – was to defend the Bible accounts of Christ's resurrection, by comparing them with the lies of Watergate.

'We couldn't hold our stories together for three weeks under that pressure,' he says, pointing by contrast to the forty years in which the disciples of Jesus never backed down on their witness to the resurrection, despite persecution and martyrdom. Colson goes on:

> 'I was around the most powerful men in the world, but we couldn't hold the lie. If the resurrection wasn't true, those disciples could never have held out. No one could do that. Someone would have dug out the tape, or something!' (*Evangelism Today* magazine, December 1984)

But no-one ever did. At times there have been those – even within church circles – who have suggested that what happened at Easter was no more than the living on of Christ's memory and influence; that, indeed, it was this that gave significance to the early Christian preaching.

We would want to ask: Have these theorists ever tried to preach such a message evangelistically? Let them try! Would anyone be changed at all, let alone a pagan continent? We must remember that there were no media to carry the news of Christ's resurrection in that first-century culture. Had the claim of Jesus' bodily rising had no foundation, the most that could have been hoped for would be a lingering wistfulness following the death of a local hero; the chalking-up of a name over a railway bridge. 'James Dean lives.' 'Elvis lives.' Perhaps for a generation a bit of folklore about a Galilean wonder-worker would have persisted – and then even the name Jesus itself, like a child's brave sandcastle on the beach, would have become washed over, rounded off and finally flattened out as though it had never been. There would not even have been a footnote in history; we should never have heard of him.

As it turned out, it was the Caesars who got flattened. To quote Andrew Knowles:

> In years to come, people would call their dogs 'Caesar', and their sons 'Matthew'. Just one of the changes Jesus makes! (*The Way Out*, Collins).

Another king? Why is this concept so threatening to some? After all, the kingdom headed by Jesus in no way assumes the place of a nation or state; it makes no territorial claim and boasts no economic or financial muscle.

When Christ began to minister in Galilee, he was clearly establishing, in his challenging of the demonic underworld, a bridgehead against the kingdom of evil. Surely there ought to have been universal gratitude that here was evident proof that goodness was stronger than evil?

The answer is that the authoritative teaching of Jesus flies in the face of all that is supposed to be politically correct. Here is a kingdom that sets before people the highest of all loyalties. Its King has set, in the Sermon on the Mount, the highest – and most radical – of all ethical standards. By his life and death he has set the entire human race the highest of all examples. And he will preside, in the final universal judgment, over the highest – the supreme – of all courts. Every individual who has ever lived will give an account to *him*.

Think of it, if you can! Congressmen and senators, Members of Parliament and county councillors; monarchs, tyrants and presidents; bishops, gurus and imams; High Court judges, lecturers, fashion designers, news announcers, generals, road sweepers, high-school students, film-makers, the literate and the illiterate, the blasphemous and the religious – all will be faced with Jesus Christ when his final universal reign is ushered at his return.

His return? Yes, politically very incorrect! There is scarcely an institution in any country of our world that isn't embarrassed by talk of 'another king' and of his kingdom that is for ever.

But we have not yet attempted a proper definition of the kingdom. Can it ever be done? Let us begin the attempt in the next chapter.

5

Seven False Views

> The disciples came to him and asked, 'Why do you
> speak to the people in parables?'
>
> He replied, 'The knowledge of the secrets of the
> kingdom of heaven has been given to you, but not
> to them.' (Matthew 13:10-11)

A puff of smoke blew into my face.

'Go on then,' said my inquisitor. He jabbed his
pipe at my chest. 'Who was Cain's wife?'

I was leading a mission in Britain's West Country,
and a group of us were sitting in someone's living-
room for a discussion. Up now popped the hoary
trick question of Cain's wife! Of course I knew that
the answer lay in Genesis 5:4, but there was no need
to reveal my hand yet.

'Cain's wife?' I repeated. 'That can't be a real
problem to you.'

'Oh yes it is! It worries me to bits!'

'Not so much that it prevents you from being a
believer.'

'It does!' A triumphant smile. 'So tell me now –
who was Cain's wife?'

'All right,' I said. 'If I give you an answer – to your intellectual satisfaction – will you become a Christian tonight?'

Scenting danger, my critic wobbled.

'Come on,' I remonstrated. 'If you walked out into the street and someone asked, "Could you tell me the way to Taunton? Of course I'm not going to Taunton, and as soon as you tell me the way I shall only turn on my heel and walk in the opposite direction – but could you tell me the way to Taunton?" what would you think of such a question? This', I went on, 'is exactly your approach. You're just playing games.'

Discussion continued, and to my friend's great credit – and my infinite surprise – he became a Christian later that night. He was to become one of the leaders in his church.

On the whole, Christian people tend to answer the questions of unbelievers a little too speedily!

As we read the Gospels, it becomes apparent that Jesus hardly ever answered a direct question. Frequently he would turn the question round.

Much of his teaching was presented in such a way that it sifted out the genuine seekers after truth from the casual triflers. Again and again the mechanism that he employed was the telling of a parable.

The parables of the kingdom were told, not to stop people from understanding the truth, but to act as a sieve among the hearers, to test inward attitudes. To understand and receive the truth is more a matter of the heart than the head. The parables were a way of saying, 'How much do you want the kingdom?' The careless debater or the professional heckler was unlikely to get past the externals of the story; the real point would pass him by – and that would be God's judgment upon him:

'In them is fulfilled the prophecy of Isaiah:

"You will be ever hearing but never understanding;
     you will be ever seeing but never perceiving.
For this people's heart has become calloused"'
                                        (Matthew 13:14-15)

The kingdom of God! Can anyone understand it? Why the fuss, in any case? The answer lies in the high profile given to it by the world's greatest teacher. Because it touches every part of life, we've only to get the teaching wrong or to distort it, and we shall land ourselves in a traffic jam of errors. Get the kingdom wrong, and we'll get politics, education and health wrong – together with sport, sex, wealth creation, the work ethic, war, social justice, race, the whole shooting-match.

This being so, why don't we begin with some false views of the kingdom? Again and again people have formed their own image of what the kingdom of God is supposed to be. So there has to be a corrective element in the teaching of the Bible. What are these false views of the kingdom? Here are seven main areas of error.

The error of nationalism

Take the Jewish zealots of Jesus' day. Of course, they claimed a religious basis for their nationalist activities – but it was really a political kingdom that they were working for; a kingdom to be established if necessary by the sword. Their rallying cry was a call to overthrow the Roman empire – and of course the hope of many, as Jesus rode into Jerusalem on Palm Sunday, was that his was such an enterprise.

There is a difference between a healthy patriotism and the grabbing nationalism that from the tower of Babel onwards ('Let us make a name for ourselves') desires to be top dog in the world. In the middle of the English Civil War, John Milton, referring to the action of God in history, asked, 'What does He then – but reveal himself to his servants, and, as his manner is, first to his Englishmen?' That is ugly enough. Let nationalist dreams be allied to religious fervour as in so many parts of the world today, and Blaise Pascal's observation of the seventeenth century becomes hideously true: 'Men never do evil so completely and cheerfully as when they do it from religious conviction' (Pascal's *Pensées*: appendix). The missing dimension in the nationalist error is the universal nature of God's kingdom; it stands astride every nation in sight.

The error of sectarianism

The sectarian mind-set equates the kingdom with its own little religious side-show. 'Come over here,' it says. 'Join us, and you'll find the kingdom!'

In Jesus' time it tended to be the Pharisees who imagined that they had the kingdom of God safely bottled up in their own system, in their codes of practice and their religious traditions. All else were excluded. Jesus had only to identify a believing Roman centurion as a member of the kingdom, to expose the falsehood:

> 'I tell you the truth, I have not found anyone in Israel with such great faith. I say to you that many will come from the east and the west, and will take their places at the feast with Abraham, Isaac and Jacob in the kingdom of heaven. But the subjects of the kingdom will be thrown outside, into the darkness, where there will be weeping and gnashing of teeth' (Matthew 8:10-12).

The implication is very clear: faith in Jesus the King, wherever it comes from, will secure a place at the Messiah's banquet. There always have been those who think that they have a natural right of access. Not so – there is a personal dimension to the kingdom, centering in Jesus, its head.

Traditional Roman Catholic theologians have tended to equate the kingdom of God with the Roman Catholic Church; but Jesus, in his kingly rule, is bigger than any church. Today we have many religious and semi-Christian groups, meeting in their own exclusive corner of God's universe, addressing only each other in the belief that nobody else matters outside of themselves.

The church is certainly closely involved in God's kingdom; to it has been entrusted the keys of the kingdom (Matthew 16:18-19); but the actual scope of the kingdom is wider than the church. Ultimately it extends to the whole of the created order when all things will be under the feet of Christ (1 Corinthians 15:27).

They couldn't see it, most of them. Nicodemus, who came by night to visit Jesus, was slow to grasp that being in the kingdom meant being born spiritually as a person, from above, by the inward working of the Holy Spirit. There is this personal aspect of the kingdom – centering in faith in Jesus – that the sectarian mentality can't take in. Hence the unbelievable fragmentation and subdivisions among many Christians today. In group after group it is a case of, 'Come over to us; we've got it all here!' All they have done is to reduce Jesus and the kingdom to the size of a small village with its own chieftain.

The error of pietism

It was May 2001, and some of us were holding a dinner party in London for 'African Enterprise'. Its founder, Michael Cassidy of South Africa was our guest speaker; he was passing through London. The issue of African genocide came up. How could Rwanda, a land of so many churches, fall prey to this terrible evil during the 1990s?

Michael put forward a possible explanation:

'Salvation was preached in Rwanda and its neighbouring territories for many decades. Thousands were won to faith, but we must ask whether we have been lacking in a proper, rounded preaching of the Kingdom.'

What Michael Cassidy said made sense. It is always possible, given the breath-taking joy of personal salvation, that the far-reaching social implications of the kingdom of God – highlighted in the thunderous tirades of the prophet Amos – can become lost in the worship, the singing and the joy of a solitary faith that fails to engage with the ills of the outside world. The Bible had something to say about this in the days of Amos:

> Away with the noise of your songs!
> I will not listen to the music of your harps.
> But let justice roll on like a river,
> righteousness like a never-failing stream!
> (Amos 5:23-24)

One of the great hallmarks of the kingdom is that of righteousness – with which Israel's Messiah would be expected to act on behalf of the poor (Isaiah 11:4). There is no mandate for a privatized kingdom of piety, where the social element is missing.

The error of humanism

Then there is an opposite tendency, where *everything* is social. In its modern form it is the product of secular humanism. Human-based in its thinking, it tends to conceive of the kingdom of God in materialistic, socio-political and economic terms. Its chief error is to belittle the spiritual nature of Christ's kingly rule (John 18:36).

There is also the teaching of liberation theology, which emerged in the second half of the twentieth century from a largely Roman Catholic, Latin-American background. We can only sympathize with its leaders, in their indignation at the terrible poverty and gross inequalities that provoked them to write. What they tended to come up with, however, was a distortion of the Bible' s message. Their key text was the book of Exodus, which was filtered through the screen of their social analysis of society, its message being presented as a liberation from political oppression.

If you misuse the Bible, you can make it mean anything! In such a case, 'the kingdom of God' can be interpreted – as it is by some – in terms of a political revolution or a well-organized factory. A well-run factory can, perhaps, exhibit some of the values of the kingdom, but it can't really be described *as* the kingdom. The kingdom of God is spiritual in nature.

The error of dualism

On an overseas visit, I found myself in a meeting where the leader announced that an evil spirit had come and inhabited the town. Hence, he said, the growing evil of the neighbourhood and the powerlessness of the church.

'Who will come to fast and pray with me?' he asked the members of the meeting. 'We need to receive a word of divine knowledge about the centre of the demon's activity, and so confront it.'

It was good that the leader took evil seriously. But an exaggerated view of 'territorial spirits' can too easily elevate the kingdom of darkness to a level virtually on a par with the kingdom of God. We are wrong to think of two parallel and eternal kingdoms, fighting it out – with the saints of God tipping the balance if they fulfil certain disciplines. For dualism, as it is called, finds no substantial support in the Scriptures. It is God's kingdom alone that is permanent and eternal.

It is perfectly true that the believer is up against 'the world', 'the flesh' and 'the devil' in the spiritual battle. The tendency in some quarters, however, is to take these three categories, and lump them all within a single camp – that of the devil alone! But that is to focus altogether too much on the devil and his kingdom. This is the age of the gospel, when our focus should emphatically be upon the rule of God and the victory of Christ over the kingdom of darkness through the cross.

The dualistic error unintentionally diverts attention from the gospel. The only hope for the world of demons is if we Christians become so mesmerized with what the demonic world is doing that we forget the power and the preaching of the cross. It is the cross that secured our victory some 2,000 years ago.

My own missionary parents worked for some years in a region of Africa that was noted for its demonic activity and the fear of the witchdoctor. But they needed no special word of divine knowledge as to what to do. They knew already that the preaching of the cross spells out the triumph of God's rule in Christ. The preaching of the cross is what they gave themselves to. A flourishing Bible School today exists in the place of their labours. Whatever happened to the evil spirits? They simply died of neglect!

The error of triumphalism

We have to beware, however, of veering in the opposite direction, and becoming so victory-conscious that we become victims of an unreal triumphalism, and forget the sacrificial aspect of the kingdom of God. James and John, disciples of Jesus, blatantly asked him whether, in the glory, they might sit on either side of him in a blaze of prominence. Our Lord had to speak to them about the cup of suffering that he would be required to accept, and that would come their way as well (Mark 10:37-38).

Too frequently we, Christ's followers, prefer to rattle our spiritual sabres, march our way to victory, and somehow persuade the world to accept the faith by the size of our marches and the loudness of our songs!

As the Danish philosopher Søren Kierkegaard once observed, '10,000 lips, shouting the same thing, make the statement fraudulent, even if it happens to be true.' He meant that the triumphalist approach runs against the style of the Messiah's kingdom: 'He will not shout or cry out, or raise his voice in the streets' (Isaiah 42:2).

Marches or large gatherings that bring spiritual encouragement need not be erased from the kingdom's agenda, but we should not delude ourselves into thinking that the power resides in the march as such. History tells us that Christianity has always touched bottom in its attempts to win the world when it was trying to be powerful, as in the period of the Crusades. It is when we know ourselves to be weak and vulnerable that God can use us powerfully.

The error of liberalism

I'll never forget my first conscious encounter with a liberal teacher of theology. I was at college and embarking on a theological degree, my ultimate aim being the Christian ministry. I had written my first essay for my new tutor, and turned up at the appointed hour for the tutorial. I was just naïve enough to expect from him some reverence for the text of Scripture. Instead he ripped into it – and me – with all the confident expertise of a long-practised demolition contractor. Naturally I was completely unequipped to challenge his extreme dogmatism – for he was dogmatic to the point of being fundamentalist in his liberalism! He was right and I was wrong – and so was the Scripture, in its 'original' meaning, its 'natural' meaning and its 'general' meaning!

I remember thinking, 'This man doesn't seem to know the Lord. I wonder if he has a daily Quiet Time? I know he is wrong, but I don't yet know why.' I resolved that one day I would equip myself to answer his arguments. I then went off to practise my tennis volleys.

Malcolm Muggeridge once wrote of what he called 'the liberal death-wish'. He commented:

> It is indeed among Christians themselves that the final assault on Christianity has been mounted. All they had to show was that when Jesus said his Kingdom was not of this world he *meant* that it was (*Conversion*, Collins).

Liberal teaching is really shown up in its unbelief when it comes to the study of eschatology – the 'last things' (Greek, *eschatos* – 'last'). Our biblical understanding is that the kingdom of God will not reach complete fulfilment (nor will the destruction of sickness, sin and death) until 'the end', when Christ returns in universal power and glory and 'hands over the kingdom to God the Father' (1 Corinthians 15:24).

The liberal error at this point is one of 'over-realized eschatology'. It denies a second coming that is yet to be – making the claim that everything that is promised has already happened, that nothing more remains.

In a strange way some of us evangelicals are prone to this error, but for a different reason. In our very eagerness to see the ultimate banishment of sickness and poverty, we have at times tried to anticipate the arrival of the kingdom's completion ahead of time. Hence the emphasis, in some quarters, on healing and perfect health *now*, and the absence of privation and tears, as part of the gospel package to be claimed by the believer in this life. The 'prosperity gospel' of recent years has arisen as a result of this misunderstanding of the eschatological nature of the kingdom, the 'not yet' aspect that we have to live with.

To conclude

We have covered a lot of ground in this chapter, so it will help to summarize these seven false views:

• The error of nationalism, failing to recognize the *universal* aspect of the kingdom.

• The error of sectarianism, with its inadequate view of the *personal* centre of the kingdom – Jesus himself.

• The error of pietism, with its deficient *social* emphasis.

- The error of humanism, blinkered to the *spiritual* nature of the kingdom.

- The error of dualism, with its failure to recognize the *eternal* nature of the kingdom.

- The error of triumphalism, with its reduced concept of the *sacrificial* nature of the kingdom.

- The error of liberalism, with its loss of the *eschatological* or future dimension of the kingdom.

So many errors! No wonder that an enormous proportion of Christ's teaching was taken up with the kingdom and its true nature. It is from the area of denying the false views that we now turn, as we try, first, to *describe* the kingdom of God, and then to *define* it.

6

The Enigma Of The Kingdom

> After John was put in prison, Jesus went into
> Galilee, proclaiming the good news of God. 'The
> time has come,' he said. 'The kingdom of God is
> near. Repent and believe the good news!'
>
> (Mark 1:14-15)

In the whole world, I can't think of a better setting
for the delivering of a series of Bible studies than
the Victoria Falls in Zimbabwe. Having been involved
in the mission work of African Enterprise for some
years, it had fallen to me to take the studies at the
International Partnership conference – and on this
occasion we'd converged at the sensational Victoria
Falls. Of course I rang home the first night.

'Have you seen it?' I heard at the other end.

'Yes,' I replied.

'Have you photographed it?'

'Yes!'

'All of it?'

'That's impossible,' I protested. 'You don't know what you're asking. It's the greatest thing I've ever seen. It's a mile across!'

What I brought back home eventually was a series of snapshots. Looked at together, I hoped that they would convey something of the majestic brilliance of that scene in Africa.

This has to be our approach when we come to the teaching of Jesus about the kingdom of God. It is so all-encompassing that a single cameo is unable to do it justice. As a result, what we are presented with is an album of stories about the kingdom – and plenty of them – each presenting basically a single facet of the great subject.

Readers of the New Testament will search in vain for a single definition of the kingdom in Jesus' teaching. Instead he would say, 'You're interested in the kingdom of God? Well :

- 'It's like someone sowing seed.

- 'It's like good seed growing alongside weeds.

- 'It's like a tiny grain of mustard seed that grew into a huge tree.

- 'It's like yeast, working its way steadily through the dough.

- 'It's like a field containing a treasure trove that a man blew all his savings on so as to acquire it.

- 'It's like the dealer in pearls who sold up everything when he finally got the chance to buy the Big One.

- 'It's like a great catch of fish that ultimately had to be sorted into the acceptable and the rejects.

And that's from the thirteenth chapter of Matthew alone! I love the touch at the end of the section, when Jesus asked his listeners, 'Have you understood all these things?'

'Yes,' they replied!

But of course they hadn't. We have only to read Acts 1:6, when – even after the miracle of the resurrection – we find the disciples saying, 'Lord, are you at this time going to restore the kingdom to Israel?'

They're still on the nationalist error; we feel like sacking the lot of them! But if, two thousand years later, people still find it hard to grasp what the kingdom of God is all about, we shouldn't feel too surprised if the disciples, in those early, heady days, were slow on the uptake.

Learning from the parables of Jesus, what can we understand of this enigma of the kingdom? The picture begins to build up:

- The kingdom has small beginnings.

- It advances slowly and unspectacularly.

- It works in an unseen way, like the yeast in dough.

- It grows side by side with evil and error.

- Its members are drawn from every part, for it is a universal kingdom.

- When discovered, it is the source of true joy and fulfilment.

- It out-prices everything else in sight.

- It requires sacrifice and surrender.

- It culminates in an eternal separation of the good from the evil, of the true from the false.

And notice how the kingdom centres in a person. That, too, was beginning to emerge during Jesus' ministry. Peter, James and John had a glimpse, a preview in miniature, of the kingdom and its glory, as witnesses of Christ in transfigured splendour (Luke 9:28-36). At the cross, the real nature of the kingdom and the mission of the King was to come into its clearest focus. The resurrection would vindicate the

King's mission. The ascension would celebrate it. The gift of the Spirit at Pentecost would broaden its impact to a world-wide dimension.

And still we go on praying, 'Your kingdom come.' Yes, it came in power with Jesus – and yet it must continue to advance until the final winding-up of history. All nations will then be subject to it. And all of the cosmos, our decaying fallen world, will become part of the complete rule of God over everything that has been chaotic.

Christ's walking on the water, healing of the sick, multiplying of the loaves – all these were indications of the final subjugation of nature, universally, which is yet to be. They were the pointers!

Is this the kingdom, though? There were many at the time of Jesus who had their doubts. Even John the Baptist, in the isolation of prison, needed some reassurance (Matthew 11:2-6). Yet from the beginning, Jesus had made plain that it was on!

'The time has come. The kingdom of God is near. Repent and believe the good news!' (Mark 1:15)

'The time has come' – or, more literally, 'Fulfilled is the time.' Here was no prophet, announcing a future kingdom and its leader. The prophets had done their part. Here at last was the reality, and it centred in the speaker.

It is at this point that the truth of the kingdom begins to glow in the life of a believer. There are really three exercises that seem to be necessary in coming to an understanding of the nature of God's kingdom:

- First to *deny*, as we look at false interpretations.

- Second to *describe*, as we deduce from the 'snapshots' in Christ's teaching what the kingdom is like.

- Third, to *define*, as now we come to what is distinctive about the kingdom.

It was May Day some years ago and I was baptizing a Communist in our church of All Souls, Langham Place! A journalist by profession, he told the crowded church, 'All my life I've been living and working for another kingdom. Today I tell you that I transfer my allegiance to a different kind of kingdom – and to a new leader, Jesus Christ.' And then he hugged me.

It is Christ indeed who gives concrete substance and significance to what it means, actually to enter the kingdom, to accept it, to become a part of it.

As we study the Bible, we begin to become aware that the vast bulk of the teaching about the kingdom of God occurs in the four Gospels. Once we get into the New Testament letters, the references to the kingdom are dramatically reduced – and yet it is the letters that provide the basic vital teaching for entire churches. Why this change in emphasis?

It simply cannot be that the apostles, Peter, Paul, John and James, diluted our Lord's teaching. Rather, what happened is what was already beginning to feature in the ministry of Jesus himself – namely that *the kingdom of God has become inseparable from the person of Christ the King.*

To come to know Christ, to grow in likeness to him, to walk in his Spirit, to make him the Lord of our lives is to have become members of the kingdom.

Let us compare some parallels in the gospels and the New Testament letters:

• For example, we read in Mark 15:43 that Joseph of Arimathea was 'waiting for the kingdom of God'. But come to the letters, and we learn that believers in Christ 'eagerly await a Saviour' (Philippians 3:20).

• Again, in the Gospels, Jesus declared that 'the kingdom of God is near' (Mark 1:15). But the letters assure us that 'the Lord's coming is near' (James 5:8).

We also learn this: that the blessings of the kingdom and the blessings of salvation are, in the end, one and the same thing. Look at the parallels:

• In Mark 10:23-25, three times Jesus tells his disciples how hard it is for certain people 'to enter the kingdom of God'. The disciples then look at each other and ask, 'Who then can be saved?' (10:26).

The implication in the conversation was that to be in the kingdom of God was to be saved.

•   Again, when speaking of the end times, Jesus, in Luke 21:31, speaks of the signs that indicate that 'the kingdom of God is near'. But in referring to the same signs he also says that his followers can raise their heads 'because your redemption is drawing near' (21:28).

So do we have, at last, a definition of 'the kingdom' in those letters? I rather think we do. In the only mention of 'the kingdom' in the entire letter to the Romans, the apostle Paul makes a statement:

> For the kingdom of God is not a matter of eating and drinking, but of righteousness, peace and joy in the Holy Spirit.   (Romans 14:17)

But what exactly is 'righteousness, peace and joy in the Holy Spirit'? Why, it's the experience of salvation! It's what every believer has stepped into, on being accepted by Christ at the cross.

You can be an illiterate, an unknown, a victim of child abuse or a prisoner in jail – but if God has met you at the cross (and he won't meet you anywhere else), you are a member of the eternal kingdom, with all the privileges that go with it.

My mother, as a missionary, years ago, was interviewing an elderly African widow for Christian baptism. The candidate was a picture of frailty, with a shawl draped over her head, obscuring her face from view. She had never had any education at all. My mother was doing her best.

'Tell me what you can about the story of Jesus.'

A shake of the head. 'It's no use asking me any questions: I'm old, ill and tired.'

'But just something to give me an idea. Tell me something that Jesus did, can you?'

'No, there's nothing that I can think of. Why bother me like this?'

'Think for a minute now. Can you tell me the name of Jesus' mother?'

At that point my brother Peter came round the corner of the house on his bicycle. Hearing the question, he chirped into the candidate's ear as he raced by, 'Mary!'

A mumble, 'Mary.'

'Well, yes. But my little boy had to tell you that'. A pause. 'I wonder whether it would be an idea to delay baptism for a while? Until perhaps you have a deeper understanding of Christian things? It would be a pity if you were baptized without an experience and testimony of Jesus.'

At the word 'testimony', there was a reaction. The old woman flung the shawl off her head, and stared with indignant eyes at her inquisitor.

'Testimony?' she repeated. 'You say I have no testimony? How can you say that, when I know in my heart how I've been freed from the world of spirits? How by the blood of Calvary I've come out of darkness into light and into the forgiveness of all

81

my sins? How I've been saved and filled with the Holy Spirit? How can you say I have no testimony? Why shouldn't I be baptized?'

The reply couldn't come fast enough. 'You can be baptized!'

Membership of the kingdom; it's the same for people of every background. *The kingdom is the rule of God through Christ the King, in the hearts and lives of his followers.* And to be a member of the kingdom is to possess the kingdom. The whole outfit! The ancient prophet Daniel said so (Daniel 7:18). So did the Christian apostle Paul:

> All things are yours, whether Paul or Apollos or Cephas or the world or life or death or the present or the future, all are yours; and you are Christ's; and Christ is God's.   (1 Corinthians 3:21-23, RSV)

We need the last phrase, 'Christ is God's', in order to tie up the whole argument. Otherwise the suggestion might be put forward that Christ was just one among a number of alternatives, a leader of yet one more religious faction. But no. The statement is clear enough – Christ is part of the very Godhead. He is the explanation of the entire universe. You belong to him? Then you have everything.

Part Three

Heralding The Kingdom

If you look at the ministry of the apostles, you will see that it is characterised by reckless faith. They were not daunted by flogging or threats or social ostracism. The truth in their hearts burned so joyfully bright that nothing else mattered.

(George Verwer, *No Turning Back*,
Hodder & Stoughton)

7

It's All About The Centre

'Not everyone who says to me, "Lord, Lord," will
enter the kingdom of heaven, but only he who
does the will of my Father who is in heaven. Many
will say to me on that day, "Lord, Lord, did we not
prophesy in your name, and in your name drive out
demons and perform many miracles?" Then I will
tell them plainly, "I never knew you. Away from
me, you evildoers!"' (Matthew 7:21-23)

Two hundred years ago there was a German
theologian called Schleiermacher. I had to study his
work at college. He once made the unusual claim
that Prussia could truly be equated with the kingdom
of God! This, he said, was on the grounds that it
was not possible to have a more civilized society
than his own at that point of history.

Others since then have adopted similar outlooks.
Kwame Nkrumah was the head of state of the
newly-independent African country of Ghana in the
1960s. The large statue of him that was erected in
the capital Accra bore an inscribed distortion of

Matthew 6:33. It read, SEEK YE FIRST THE POLITICAL KINGDOM.

Amsterdam 2000 was the contrast. It was Millennium year, and Billy Graham had invited some 11,000 of us preaching evangelists to the great Europa Hall at the RAI Centre in Amsterdam, a city of canals and bicycles. The eight-day Congress could have been filled three times over, had there been space, so great was the flood of applicants for places As it was, we were drawn from no less than 209 countries. Neither the United Nations nor the Olympic Games have ever matched such a spread of nations. Amsterdam 2000 was the most internationally-representative gathering, secular or religious, in all of history.

Totally absent were the tensions between cultures and nationalities. From day one there descended upon the Chinese and Russians, upon the South Americans and North Americans, upon the Africans, Antipodeans, Asians and Europeans, a holy unity that had only one explanation - expressed in our final service of Holy Communion - and that was the overall kingship of Jesus Christ. We were there for him, ready to be re-commissioned for the twenty-first century as ambassadors of his kingdom; preparing to fan out once more to decaying democracies, traumatised war-zones, anti-Christian regimes and the world's ash-heaps of lawlessness, street children and HIV.

A meeting of the world's evangelists is always going to be more decisive for the future of the world than any G8 Summit. The kingdom of God – the only entity that will still be there at the end – has as its key representatives, not the political or military players of history, but those who can genuinely be said to be ambassadors of its divine king.

What kind of people are these? What is the life-style that stamps their identity? Jesus gives the answer in the most influential public utterance ever delivered – the Sermon on the Mount:

...The salt of the earth...hiding your light....an eye for an eye....turning the other cheek....casting your pearls before swine....building on sand – these and other phrases from Christ's unforgettable words have passed into the daily idioms and expressions of people everywhere.

The actor, Robert Powell, who played the part of Christ in Zeffirelli's film *Jesus of Nazareth*, said later,

> 'The setting was superb and I got carried away. The beauty of the words and ideas, when spoken aloud, are overwhelming. Half way through I started crying.... You can read the words in the Bible, but when you come to say them aloud, it's something else. They are electric' (*Daily Express*, 26.1.1977).

Matthew 5-7 provides us with three of the most disturbing chapters in the Bible. They are not telling us how to be saved. They are giving the reader a portrait – a CV – of the life that is expected of the saved person! You have been saved? Forgiven? You have entered the kingdom of God? Then begin to live like one of its ambassadors!!

Some have despaired that such a life is liveable. But the fact that there are people whom we have met, who have reminded us in their character and life-style of Christ – himself being the supreme model of such living – makes the point clear enough. And the big point that comes through is that the kingdom of God is to be defined by its centre, not by its circumference. On the circumference of the crowds that came to hear Jesus were the Pharisees – and they lived life on the circumference too. Theirs was the way of outward religion. Their almsgiving, praising, praying, fasting and serving were shot through with self-promotion – here was a way of life instantly recognizable by the public for its observable activity. But these religious practitioners were oblivious to the central Kingship to which they owed their hearts' allegiance.

What is going on in the heart, the inner motivation and conscience? The points spill out from the teaching of Jesus:

- Give secretly, not publicly (Matthew 6:2-4).

- Praise privately, not ostentatiously (v.5-8).

- Fast quietly, not hypocritically (v.16-18).

- Focus eternally, not selfishly (v.19-23).

- Serve single-mindedly, not dividedly (v.24).

- Live trustingly, not materialistically (v.25-34).

- Judge humbly, not vindictively (7:1-5).

All this ran precisely against the values operated by the Pharisees. No-one can serve two masters, said Jesus. But the Pharisees made the attempt – God and themselves! Ultimately it can only be one or the other, and humanity has to choose. Which master will we be found identified with at the last day? It's one or the other; it's kill or cure. There are the two crowds of Matthew 7:13 and 14, the true and the false prophets of vv.15-23, the good and the bad fruit of vv.17-20, and the two houses of vv.24-27. The passage is filled with warnings.

It's only a matter of time – the sure judgment of God will determine who was living life on the circumference, and who at the centre. Appearances and claims amount to nothing under the scrutiny of God. In Matthew 7:22,23, Jesus warns of those who, at the final judgment, will plead for entrance to the kingdom, on the ground of their religious activities, carried out even in his name. It all looks sensational enough:

- Prophecy
- Exorcism
- Miracles

But because the interests of the King himself were not at the heart of their loyalty and affections, they will be turned away as 'evildoers'.

It's terrifying. There are those who make the facile claim, 'The Sermon on the Mount – that stuff about Love your Neighbour – is all the religion we need'. Such discipleship hasn't even left the starting gate; it's still on the circumference of the kingdom and its issues. It is as incongruous to tag a virtue of Christ onto your lifestyle as it is to tie an orange onto an orange tree and expect it to grow. Good fruit comes from a good tree – it doesn't come from nowhere. Jesus said so – in the Sermon:

> By their fruit you will recognise them. Do people pick grapes from thornbushes, or figs from thistles? Likewise every good tree bears good fruit, but a bad tree bears bad fruit. A good tree cannot bear bad fruit, and a bad tree cannot bear good fruit.
>
> (Matthew 7:16-18)

As Europe – with most of the West – busies itself with throwing out the Biblical principles that provided its cultural unity from the start, there are desperate attempts being made to acquire some kind of pragmatic form of decent citizenship that is nevertheless divorced from its Christian origins. These attempts will fail. If it's quality fruit that you're looking for, it can only be produced from within membership of the kingdom of God. This whole issue is all about the centre!

The wooden moralism of the Pharisees reduced the living ethics of the Old Testament to a dry system that fitted their own traditions – leaving out the heart and the centre. So they hadn't committed murder? Or adultery? Wrong. What is portrayed on the video film of the heart is as real to God as the physical action. Jesus always went to the heart. You want to see the hallmark of true radical discipleship? Then love your enemies – and become part of a blazing comet trail across the face of history!

Some listeners to Jesus' words, as he presented the highest ethical standards ever advocated, might have wilted, and felt their case was hopeless. This is why the 'Ask...seek....knock' of Matthew 7:7-11 fits so perfectly into the sermon. How to live according to the opening Beatitudes of chapter 5? How to live, witness and preach with integrity; how to avoid the pitfalls, to escape the charge of hypocrisy, to live always in the light of judgment – why, it seems beyond anyone to steer a straight and responsible course.

But it is very simple in reality. We have only to get our motives clear and our direction true....and 'ask'. The tense of the original Greek indicates that we are to keep on asking and knocking – and this fits in precisely with the theme of the parable of Luke 11: 5-10, which neatly precedes the parallel passage to Matthew of asking, seeking and knocking. In the Luke parable, the visitor at midnight obtains the loan of bread from his reluctant neighbour, despite the late hour, the locked door and the sleeping household – because he persisted.

The emphasis in that parable lies in its contrast. God is utterly unlike the man in bed! He is not a lender in any case; he's a giver. The door is never locked, on God's part. And, to God, it is never midnight! All the more reason, then, to persist in our heartfelt desire to enter into the true life of his kingdom.

For God wants to give to those who ask him (Matthew 6:9-11). He is not a security guard; he is not an official asking for your pass; it is the 'Father' to whom you come. Will a true father hand out bogus, trick presents? Does he perpetrate jokes on his children? Will he hand over a stone, camouflaged to look like a hamburger? Will he serve up a snake, when they'd asked for some tilapia fish?

Ask for his help, says Jesus. The way of the kingdom is not lived on the circumference, but at the centre – where the King is. Only then can we be his ambassadors, successfully threading our way through the twenty-first century maze. The model has already been given us in the Sermon.

And those Beatitudes with which the Sermon began, at the start of chapter 5 – that is what you are going to look like, if you follow this King. No, the Beatitudes are not an entrance exam that has to be passed! They are the fruit that Christ will cause his followers to bear. In this the Beatitudes represent a promise rather than a command:

• Blessed are the poor in spirit, for theirs is the kingdom of heaven.

• Blessed are those who mourn, for they will be comforted....

There is a progression in those first ten verses of Matthew 5 – first, understanding our need and sinfulness; then desiring the righteousness of God – and moving finally to serving him, through persecution. This is the 'blessed' life, the 'happy' life. *But we must understand 'happy' here, not primarily from our point of view, but from God's!* When saved people are living the true life of the kingdom, their 'happy' state is something that he pronounces on them – much as in Psalm 1:1, 'Blessed is the man who does not walk in the counsel of the wicked.'

Some Christian writing has, perhaps, unwittingly distorted the nature of the Beatitudes by such titles as, 'The Secret of a Happy Life'. Subconsciously the reader begins to think in terms of western therapy books; How to be Successful....How to Live a Happy Life. But Christ's Beatitudes are not tips for living. They are a portrait of what you are going to be like, in your outlook and character, if you embark upon the life of the kingdom. They will be the tell-tale signs of the gospel and its grace, that enable the King to recognize his own at the end of time. Was it a work of grace, in the last analysis? Or was it all dust and noise, and at the end the dreadful, 'I never knew you. Away from me'?

For by the end of the Sermon, Christ's listeners would have understood quite clearly that the kingdom of God centres in his own Person. Was it Me that you were serving? Was it Me that your life centred around?

Heralding the kingdom, and living its life – nothing else matters than this. It's all about the centre.

8

The Defeat Of Evil

'Now my heart is troubled, and what shall I say?
"Father, save me from this hour?" No, it was for
this very reason I came to this hour.'   (John 12:27)

The great footballer Pelé once scored such a
sensational goal that it was shown on Brazilian
television every day for a year. There were no
complaints from the viewing public.

Come to the supreme triumph of the ages – the
victory of goodness over evil at the cross of Jesus
Christ – and millions will rise up to witness that they
never tire of reviewing the event some 2,000 years
later. When did we hear of any other death that was
actually celebrated? For Christians sometimes speak
of 'a celebration of the Holy Communion'. It is the
dramatic, sacramental replay of Christ's death that
they are referring to.

Of course no camera lens of human
understanding could ever capture what was taking
place on Skull Hill, the day Jesus was crucified. The
cross itself is a lens, trained on us, examining a society
under judgment and confronting the whole apparatus

of evil created from our human revolt. The entire life and ministry of God's Messiah were focused towards this single moment. 'My hour' or 'my time' was how Jesus repeatedly referred to the coming ordeal (e.g. Matthew 26:18; John 2:4; 7:6, 8, 30).

Vast aeons had come and gone; the destiny of God's people and his kingdom had been agonizingly worked out amid the shifting fortunes of turbulent nations over many centuries. Everything was to narrow down to this one 'hour'. Once past, the programme of the kingdom would broaden again, to take in Judea, the Roman empire and ultimately the world.

The shape of kingdom history has been described as an old-fashioned hourglass, wide at each end and narrow at the centre. Initially the concept is enormous: 'God saw everything that he had made. Let us make man'. Then a nation is chosen – Israel. The narrowing increases when four fifths of the nation go into captivity, and we are left with the salvation stage-set of tiny Judea, roughly the size of Wales, or Rhode Island. It shrinks still further, because even that small remnant proves unreliable. By the time we come to the New Testament, we are down to thirteen people only – Jesus and the Twelve. Surely it can get no smaller?

But it does. The drama boils to a crisis when even that limited band comes apart, one member turning traitor, another becoming coward and the rest scattering. The narrowest part of the hourglass brings us to one individual faced with solitary degradation, deserted by all – and everything in the divine kingdom rests upon his faithfulness and sacrificial obedience.

Stephen Neill writes:

At that moment he is Israel; he is the people of God; he is the incarnation of the purpose of God with his world (*Christian Faith Today*, Pelican).

From then on the widening process of gospel proclamation begins, featuring – in ever-expanding ripples – 'Jerusalem, Judea, Samaria and the ends of the earth' (see Acts 1:8).

At the centre of everything stands the cross. Although it happened outside a single city and over the space of a few hours only, its shadow falls both forwards and backwards across the entire span of our existence. The apostle John writes of 'the Lamb that was slain from the creation of the world' (Revelation 13:8). The cross deals with the pardon even of sins that will be committed up to the end of time. It also acts retrospectively, on behalf of sinners born long before Christ's coming, who nevertheless trusted in the grace and mercy of God as they received it.

To take an obvious example, the Old Testament sacrifices had no power in themselves to deal with human guilt. They could give only temporary cover to sinful people, in anticipation of Christ's full atonement that lay ahead. We can find a parallel in modern car insurance companies who will issue a temporary 'cover note' if there is a delay in finalizing the required policy. The cover note tides matters over and keeps the car legally on the road until the document proper can be issued.

So it was with the Jewish rituals of old. They could never provide more than a temporary 'cover note' in anticipation of Christ's full and complete sacrificial death. The old system could only be 'a shadow of the good things that are coming' (Hebrews 10:1).

The death of Jesus, then, brought the age-long advance of the kingdom of God to its appointed hour of reality and of crisis.

The hour when accident and design converged
The world gasps in horror when it turns out that an innocent person has been convicted of a crime. On 9 March 1950, twenty-five-year-old Timothy Evans was hanged at London's Pentonville Prison for the murder of his wife and baby girl. He had been convicted on the evidence of John Christie, who lived in the flat beneath. When, in 1953, Christie himself was caught and then executed for the murder of his own wife and six other women, the appalling truth began to dawn that an innocent man had been executed. It took thirteen years for officialdom to admit the improbability of two mass murderers living in the same house, and a posthumous free pardon was eventually granted to poor Timothy Evans.

The Defeat Of Evil

Viewed from the standpoint of justice alone, the execution of Jesus Christ saw human wickedness and incompetence at their all-time worst. Here was the purest being that had ever walked the hills of Galilee; healer of the sick, champion of the poor – and preacher of an ethic that can never be surpassed. And yet the verdict went against him.

The trial had been a charade. A clandestine arrest, a hearing in the illegal hours of night, the fragility of the false witnesses, the collapse of the case! And yet the grim game went on, as the buck was passed from Pilate to Herod, and back again to Pilate. No sentence was ever pronounced. Yet Jesus was handed over to be crucified. Pilate's public statement was that he had found 'no basis for your charges against him'. 'Therefore,' he added, 'I will punish him and then release him' (Luke 23:14-16)!

Unbelievably unjust as it was, there was worse to come, with a kind of populist vote taking place, between the innocent Jesus and a condemned murderer, Barabbas.

Which way would we have voted? A virtuous shake of the head: 'I couldn't have voted for Barabbas.'

Don't bank on it. Put yourself in the volatile atmosphere of a football crowd. Then two candidates are presented for the popular choice: a quiet, grave, supremely good man, and a defiant, colourful rogue. The probability is that most would opt with the crowd – for the flamboyant villain. 'He may be a no-gooder,' we would say to our neighbour, 'but what a character!' Don't think that such a thing would take place only in the buzz of a sports stadium, either. The likelihood is that, put to the vote in the Union debating society of any university you care to nominate around the world, the vote would go the same way.

The crucifixion looks like the most barbarous accident of justice ever, as Jesus is put to death; seemingly a martyr to his own greatness.

But the apostolic preaching of the kingdom forcibly pointed to the divine plan that lay behind it all. Accident and design met at the cross:

> 'This man was handed over to you by God's set purpose and foreknowledge; and you, with the help of wicked men, put him to death by nailing him to the cross. But God raised him from the dead. Therefore let all Israel be assured of this: God has made this Jesus, whom you crucified, both Lord and Christ' (Acts 2:23-24, 36).

From the start, the mission of Jesus could find its completion only at the hill called Calvary. The temptation to bypass the cross was tantalizingly held out to him all along:

- • 'Throw yourself off the temple, Jesus! Astound the world; win your kingdom by popular acclaim at a single stroke!' (Matthew 4:6)
- • 'You can have the whole world. Every kingdom in sight. Just for one little bow'. (Matthew 4:8-9)

• 'It's great to have you here, miracle-worker. I'm Herod; I could get you let off. What about one little miracle for me?' (Luke 23:8-11)

Friends, disciples, relatives were all on hand, in one way or another, to divert the Messiah from his planned pathway. But Jesus wouldn't co-operate.

Then one night, in the Garden of Gethsemane, he shook his disciples into wakefulness:

'Are you still sleeping and resting? Enough! The hour has come. Look, the Son of Man is betrayed into the hands of sinners'. (Mark 14:41)

At last, human accident and divine plan were about to meet in the Son of Man's appointment with death. An 'hour' was enough for what had to be done.

The hour when evil and goodness clashed

Up to then, Jesus had spoken of the coming ordeal as 'my hour'. But as the moment approaches in the confusion of the arrest in Gethsemane, he resorts to a different expression:

'Every day I was with you in the temple courts, and you did not lay a hand on me. But this is your hour – when darkness reigns'. (Luke 22:53)

'Your hour.' All through the journey of the Bible, the decisive collision between two kingdoms had been approaching. The pace quickened as Jesus of Nazareth began his ministry in Galilee. Occult powers, hitherto entrenched, found themselves dislodged and their kingdom shaking before the authority of the Son of God:

> 'What do you want with us, Jesus of Nazareth? Have you come to destroy us? I know who you are – the Holy One of God!' (Mark 1:24)

The Bible never really gives a definitive answer as to the origin of evil. It takes evil seriously, never accommodating the errors of dualism, pessimism, romantic optimism or triumphalism. But evil is too negative, it seems, to be credited with a positive origin in its own right.

• Evil represents a defection – not a first cause. Augustine commented, 'The cause of evil is not the good, but defection from the good.'

• Evil is headed by a counterfeit, not an absolute. Satan is no more than an angel who nevertheless attempted to usurp the place that belongs to God. As a created being, his opposite is not God, but Michael, the leader of the angelic hosts. This is why it is Michael, technically, who is portrayed as defeating Satan at the time of Jesus' death (Revelation 12:7-9).

• Evil produces monotony, not creativity. In the language of Genesis 3:14-19, it can produce only dust, death, pain, thorns and thistles – in short, a wilderness. In fiction, evil frequently comes across as alive, even attractive. But real life turns the tables completely. It is goodness that proves lastingly attractive, while evil can produce only an Auschwitz, the killing-fields of Bosnia, a twisted charnel-house where New York's World Trade Centre had stood, the flattened-out grey wastelands of political or religious totalitarianism.

But evil is real all right. In Christ's terminology, Satan was 'the prince of this world', whose time was approaching when he would be 'driven out' by the power of the cross (John 12:31-33).

The cross became the focal point for the supreme effort of the kingdom of darkness. Blasphemies, hatreds, deceptions and cosmic powers converged upon the lonely figure hanging in the baking heat of a Friday afternoon. It was there that the issue of evil versus goodness was decided, through Christ's obedience to death – 'even death on a cross' (Philippians 2:8).

Representatives of the Christian gospel have every reason to encourage those who, by the power of the cross, seek freedom from demonism, witchcraft and spiritism in their many different forms. It was the historian T. R. Glover who commented that the essence of magic was to be able to link the name of a demon with the name of one's enemy – and to set the demon on that person.

'Very well,' said the Christian, 'link my name with your demons. Use my name in any magic you like. There is a name that is above every name: I'm not

103

afraid.' That put the demons in their place. Wherever
Jesus Christ has come, the demons have gone (*The
Jesus of History*, SCM Press).

Despite the fact that evil has not given up the
struggle, and will not do so until the very end, the
kingdom of God works and progresses, not *towards*
victory, but *from* the platform of victory already
achieved. This makes a great difference to the morale
of the Christian witness! The final outcome is already
assured. And all because of Christ's triumphant
'hour'.

The hour when defeat and victory coincided
'This is your hour,' Jesus had said to his arresters as
they came to take him, but it was only an hour. The
cross represents the summit of evil, but also its limit.
In the very moment of evil's triumph lay the seeds
of its overwhelming rout.

John Stott writes:

We are not to regard the cross as defeat and the
resurrection as victory. Rather, the cross was the
victory won and the resurrection the victory
endorsed, proclaimed and demonstrated (*The Cross
of Christ*, Inter-Varsity Press).

It is simply no good at all trying to understand
the victory of the cross as an outsider to the faith.
To the outsider, the death of Jesus at Jerusalem has
always looked like the end of the story. But to the

insider it *is* the story – representing, in the words of a hymn, 'His people's hope, his people's wealth, their everlasting theme.'

It is not surprising that the message of Christ's saving death has repeatedly met with mental blocks on the part of its listeners. The cross reminds us of our sin – and of our helplessness outside of God's intervention. It repels us with its image of a blood religion. It challenges us with its standard – that of self-giving service. It restricts us with its exclusive claim that there is only one ground of forgiveness. The Jews found the cross offensive; the Greeks thought it ludicrous. But as far as the New Testament apostles were concerned, the message of Christ crucified was the power and the wisdom of God (1 Corinthians 1:22-25).

This being so, it is scarcely impossible to exaggerate the power that lies in the death of the Son of God. And yet every generation will produce its crop of teachers who will speak and plan their programmes as though it were not enough to proclaim Christ crucified for our salvation. They feel obliged to introduce additional features to make the message more 'powerful' or appealing. Sometimes an evening of miracles and healing is pre-announced. The assumption is that the proclaiming of the cross cannot stand on its own.

Naturally we should be glad if there are beneficial by-products accompanying the communication of the Christian good news. When they happen, they can be gratefully received as a bonus, but in no way should they be planned for as a strategy. Many times I have observed that when they do become part of the strategy, imperceptibly they take over the central place, and the Bible and the cross become lost in an atmosphere of human-inspired hype, where the thin line between the prophetic and the hysteric has been crossed. When this happens the real and lasting power has evaporated from our message. From then on the tendency is to lurch from one extreme to the next in an insatiable quest for "power." If only we knew it, the downfall of evil at the hands of Christ is assured from one end of the Bible to the other. The whisper of it is already there in Genesis 3:15 with the hint that it will be by the seed of the woman that the serpent's head will be crushed. Here is a preview of the Christ, the 'second Adam', whose obedience in death would seal the serpent's fate.

It is there in Psalm 2, where the triumph of God's Messiah over the rebellious kings of earth is expressed in the holy laughter of heaven:

> The One enthroned in heaven laughs:
>   The Lord scoffs at them (Psalm 2:4).

Here are the defiant leaders of this world, struggling and jostling in their few short years for the number one spot. They can make us weep at times; indeed Jesus wept over the obstinacy of Jerusalem. But they don't begin to rattle the throne of God. They're laughably pathetic.

In the end it's funny-sad. 'You defy God,' says the psalmist, 'and God will make a joke of you.' Think back to the days of Egyptian power, when Pharaoh was decreeing with full solemnity that all Hebrew baby boys were to be killed at birth. If only you knew it, Pharaoh, it will be within your household that the toughest Hebrew of all will be raised and nurtured by your own daughter! Egypt would never be quite the same after Moses.

Look at Stalin, in the invincible days of the Soviet Union, stamping on the Christian church. If only you knew it, Stalin, you had a dissident in your own family! Stalin's daughter, Svetlana, who left Russia in 1967, confessed,

> 'I was brought up in a family where there was never any talk about God, but when I became a grown-up person, I found that it was impossible to exist without God in one's heart.'

It's a joke, Stalin; it's God's joke. Or take that terrible string of Caesars; godlike, all-powerful in their time. One was killed by his own son, one went mad, one went blind, one was drowned and one was strangled. Two committed suicide, five were assassinated and eight were killed in battle. One of them, Julian, as he died, gasped, 'Thou hast conquered, O Galilean.'

Years ago in America, a sports axiom ran, 'Never bet against Notre Dame, the New York Yankees or Ted Schroeder in the fifth set.' Christians, with their eye on past history, could equally assert, 'Never write off the kingdom of God before the final act' – or, to use the Bible's term, 'before Armageddon'.

It is from a lonely hilltop where a dying man's last triumphant shout was heard, 'It is finished!' that we draw our assurance that goodness will have the final word.

9

A Question Of Arithmetic

'You are those who have stood by me in my trials.
And I confer on you a kingdom'. (Luke 22:28-29)

In a radio talk I heard, James Jones, before he
had become Bishop of Liverpool, told of the
Chinese legend in which a man and wife, after many
years of longing for a child, had their desire granted.
A little boy was born to them, and they were
overjoyed. A genie then appeared and invited them
to name one wish for their baby. After careful
deliberation they spoke their minds confidently.

'We wish', they announced, 'that our child will
never experience any pain.'

'No, no!' protested the genie. 'Please! Anything
but that, I beg you!'

But the couple were adamant. 'We've thought it
all over,' they maintained, 'and this is our settled wish.'
The interview was over and the genie vanished.

It was as well that the parents never lived to see the ultimate fulfilment of their wish. Their child grew to be a terrible tyrant in the kingdom.

Every whim of his was granted; nothing was denied him. Frustration and pain never came his way and the sorrows of others meant nothing to him. No-one loved him; he had no friends. His very self-absorption was finally to become his own hell.

A strange kingdom was his. A trouble-free life? He must have been intolerable to live with. It is not that we should invite adversity upon ourselves, as did Peregrinus of old, who set fire to himself at the Olympic Games in AD 165. Trouble will come into the life of every citizen of our planet in any case. Rather, it is through how we take account of hardship, and establish its place within the framework of our world-view, that we can become prepared to face it ourselves, and confront it in the lives of others.

Here are the apostle Paul and his companion Barnabas, travelling through Asia Minor. The greatest traveller of his day, Paul has no time for sightseeing. Nor is he concerned about the quality of the local hotels; it's the state of the prisons that he has greater regard for – he knows he'll end up in them. Barnabas speaks up.

'You're a bit better now after that stoning at Lystra, aren't you? What's our topic for tonight?'

'I thought we could speak on that Greek word again, *thlipsis*. Feel up to it?'

'Oh, tribulation. Fine. We'll use the same poster the locals put up at Iconium.'

'The one with the logo of the Roman gallows?'
'That's the one. It's sure to bring in the crowds!'

They returned to Lystra and to Iconium and to Antioch, strengthening the souls of the disciples, exhorting them to continue in the faith, and saying that through many tribulations we must enter the kingdom of God (Acts 14: 21-22, RSV).

If we don't hear much of this teaching in Christian circles today, it is hardly the fault of the Bible. The New Testament is full of it. Hardship and the life of the kingdom are firmly locked into each other.

Adversity as a trademark

Tribulation (*thlipsis*) – the English itself comes from a Latin word that carries the idea of grinding, threshing, stamping, beating – and applying pressure. It's used in James 1:27 of orphans and widows in their 'distress'. It's used of material shortage in 2 Corinthians 8:13. Jesus used it of a woman in labour; she forgets her *thlipsis* for joy that her child has been born (John 16:21). It's used of the 'narrow' road that leads to life (Matthew 7:14). It's used of the 'trials' of persecution, in 1 Peter 1:6.

All the way down history, the Christian church has faced the squeezings of numerous dictatorships, the wars and mistakes of foolish and wicked people – together with the hardships associated with a fallen world. The full expectation is that, if you choose the way of Christ, life will be made uncomfortable by the squeezing pressure that will be exerted on each side of the narrow path that you tread. 'Many tribulations': life in God's kingdom will bear this trademark until Christ returns.

Adversity as a battle scar

When Paul and Barnabas stress that through many tribulations we must enter the kingdom, it is the 'must' of emphatic necessity that is used. Enduring hardship is a 'must' of discipleship! We were warned from the beginning. Jesus used the *thlipsis* word when he said, 'In this world you will have trouble' (John 16:33). Arm yourself, if you will, with the two reasons why this should be so.

First, we are called to follow in the footsteps of someone who himself was called upon to suffer.

> 'Then they will deliver you up to tribulation, and put you to death; and you will be hated by all nations for my name's sake' (Matthew 24:9, RSV).

Again and again we can expect to find ourselves on the receiving end of the anger that Christ's mission has generated.

When Mehdi Dibaj, a leading Iranian Christian, was tortured, kept in a cell measuring about one metre square, and finally sentenced to death in December 1993, he knew the reason. Brought up as a Muslim, his conversion to Christ was regarded as 'apostasy', punishable by death. 'How glorious,' he wrote from prison, 'to follow the One who has become my Saviour!' Worldwide pressure from concerned people secured Mehdi's release for a period, but the charges against him were never dropped. He was finally killed in July 1994. Earlier he had interpreted the verdict against him 'for the test of our faith to show how far we are ready to follow him'.

Those who suffer – in whatever degree – as a direct result of following Jesus Christ, will find immeasurable comfort in the knowledge that their scars, whether physical, emotional or circumstantial, are honourable scars, carried for him. Commit his words to memory:

> 'You are those who have stood by me in my trials. And I confer on you a kingdom'. (Luke 22:28-29)

Secondly, scars may be expected because God has chosen the way of hardship for our spiritual growth and advance. The newest Christian needs to be taught this, because our natural tendency – in the face of opposition – is to ask, 'Why should this be happening to me?' Our inclination is to see adversity as an interruption, and we hope that when it is over we can get back to living 'the normal Christian life'. Then we discover from the Scriptures – and we see it lived out all over the world – that adversity *is* the normal Christian life. It is the kingdom! Jesus warned us of this when, telling of the trials that his followers would face, he said,

'When you see these things happening, you know that the kingdom of God is near.' (Luke 21:31)

Festo Kivengere was a dynamic Ugandan leader whose defiance of the Amin regime culminated in his enforced exile by foot over the mountains. ('Amin couldn't guarantee my safety!') He described the pressures that he and his people underwent as 'the polishing of the saints'.

Once you see it in the New Testament, you can hardly see anything else – and you wonder how the idea ever got around that discipleship was some sort of balloon ride fuelled by 'experiences'. Why, to enter upon the life of the kingdom is to invite a whole bundle of new problems that you had never encountered before! True, the big, blockbusting problems are solved for ever at the reception of Christ's Spirit – the issue of forgiveness, relationship to God, our eternal destiny and the meaning of our existence.

But then come *thlipsis* and opposition. When young Christians at our church tell me of their new-found difficulties, I encourage them. 'It's a good sign, really,' I nod. 'It's OK – it's actually an indication that you really have made a start, and that you're growing as a Christian. It's all in the New Testament!' And it really is.

Dear friends, do not be surprised at the painful trial you are suffering, as though something strange were happening to you. But rejoice that you participate in the sufferings of Christ, so that you may be overjoyed when his glory is revealed (1 Peter 4:12-13).

'But I don't feel that I have suffered for my faith. I feel so guilty!' A woman had come up to me at the end of a meeting in Washington DC. I hastened to reassure her.

'There's no point in seeking adversity,' I explained. 'Even so, if we're not being particularly pressurized as Christians, it's an abnormal situation as compared with millions of others. In which case,' I went on, 'what you could do is to open a dossier on some part of the world where it's a real hassle to be a Christian believer. Get the prayer letters, cut out newspaper articles; in short, by your prayers, interest and support, identify with those who are your sisters and brothers in suffering.'

'I'll make a start on it today,' promised my American enquirer.

The strong probability is that, one way or another, our faith will come under pressure, and we shall be the bearers of battle scars for the cross and for the kingdom.

Adversity as a gateway

The Christian experience of progress from setback, of power through weakness, can be illustrated from 500 years ago – in the greatest man-made thing I have ever seen, Michelangelo's twice-than-life-size sculpture of David. It was in the summer of 1499 that Florence, cradle of the Renaissance and centre of European civilization, hosted a competition. Artists were invited to submit ideas for a sculpture, from a giant 17-foot high marble block that had been quarried by Agostino di Duccio.

But there was an extra challenge! The marble block had been badly gouged midway down its length, and, as expert eyes examined it, the suspicion grew that the block must inevitably break at its narrowest point. Artists, one by one, began to back out of the competition. Even the great Leonardo da Vinci declined the Duccio block. But Michelangelo, then in his twenties, stayed in the running, and finally won the commission.

The artist did his calculations – and found a way of making the weakness in the block work to his advantage. The result was the stupendous figure of David, left hand on sling-shot, eyeing Goliath as he decides to take on the giant. And there in Florence's Accademia he stands to this day. David is Michelangelo's archetypal human being, formed in the divine image; humanity at its best, symbolizing every person's moment of decision for God. My eyes mist over as I look at David, himself a giant now and all from a piece of flawed marble that others had given up on.

For this is the point in Bible terms: that the unbeliever and the Christian tend to view frustration from opposite poles. The unbeliever sees difficulty and suffering as an interruption, even as a dead end. But the Christian learns to use tribulation as a gateway, as a way out – into creativity and the very kingdom itself. Paul and Barnabas gave this message wherever they went – for it has to be taught.

Men and women who have taken God seriously have had to think out these issues. They've weighed the best that this world can offer against the hardest aspects of life in God's kingdom and when they've done their mathematics, the kingdom of God emerges as their option. Even before the time of Christ the saints of old were doing this:

> By faith Moses, when he had grown up, refused to be known as the son of Pharaoh's daughter. He chose to be ill-treated along with the people of God rather than to enjoy the pleasures of sin for a short time. He regarded disgrace for the sake of Christ as of greater value than the treasures of Egypt, because he was looking ahead to his reward (Hebrews 11:24-26).

To do your arithmetic in this way is basic to living under the rule of Jesus Christ. Unless you 'die' to self-interest, self-promotion, self-indulgence – and so take up your cross – you cannot be Christ's disciple (Luke 14:27).

It sounds like upside-down teaching. How can anyone be fulfilled by 'dying' to self? But look at it the other way. There are reminders – on every side and every day – that you can occupy the world's top spot in the field of sport, entertainment or society; you can be rich enough to be waited on hand and foot; you can be talented, personable and adored by millions – and still not be together as an integrated person. You can attain your wildest dreams, yet still not possess the 'one thing', 'the prize' of which Paul writes (Philippians 3:13-14); 'the pearl of great price' of Jesus' parable – the kingdom (Matthew 13:45-46), without which everything ultimately crumbles into meaninglessness.

The death of Christ for our sins is the way in, and, if we can only see it, adversity acts as the gateway to repentance and faith in him.

Adversity as a tutor

We can sharpen the issue by asking, 'Who are the people today who, more than any other, challenge and inspire us to a higher level of dedicated service?' Without any doubt they are those who have known, and come through, hardship at first hand.

I remember one such person vividly, Bishop Nathaniel Garang from the Southern Sudan, brought out on a visit by the Church Missionary Society. He spoke at our church one Sunday night. Ministering, as he did, in the middle of a war zone, it was assumed that he had been killed when he simply disappeared.

Five long years passed. One day, to the general astonishment of the civilised world, he reappeared like a ghost from the past, greyer and thinner, but intact. Then the pieces of his story began to come together. During those five years, he had steadily walked his way through the African bush, living off what he could as he travelled from locality to locality, encouraging scattered believers, spreading the Christian faith and establishing new churches. Phrases from the apostle Paul came into my mind as he told me his story:

> I have been constantly on the move. I have been in danger ...I have laboured and toiled and have often gone without sleep; I have known hunger and thirst and have often gone without food; I have been cold and naked. Besides everything else, I face daily the pressure of my concern for all the churches.
>
> (2 Corinthians 11:26-28)

At the beginning of the five years there had been six churches in Nathaniel's diocese. By the time he re-emerged into public view there were 250 – each of them with hundreds of members. 'You are one of the great ones of this world,' I thought. Those eyes, that had seen so much, were a message in themselves, and instilled in all who met him a feeling of 'I do not want to go on living at this level any more.'

For in true New Testament style, tribulation walks hand in hand with glory. The two go together, like bacon and egg, or strawberries and cream. Listen to Peter:

> I appeal as a fellow-elder, a witness of Christ's sufferings and one who also will share in the glory to be revealed (1 Peter 5:1).

Or listen to John:

> I, John, your brother, who share with you in Jesus
> the tribulation and the kingdom (Revelation 1:9,
> RSV).

If pain and pressure are so bound up with the kingdom, it may be asked, 'Why then do we bother?' To put it another way, 'Why become a Christian?' Is it because of the new dynamic and sense of purpose that are on offer? There is that, of course, but it is not the main reason. Because of the Christian fellowship that compensates for the hardships involved? No, not that either. Because of the exciting and uplifting experiences that may come our way? That can hardly be, in the light of Christ's firm prediction of trouble.

In the last analysis, the only reason for joining a group that will be under pressure till the end of time is that *Christianity is true*. Christ is who he claims to be!

Where then does the attraction lie? Why, the magnetism centres in the beckoning figure of Jesus himself who says, 'I've been this way ahead of you; take up your cross and follow me.' As we do so, there is a strange joy and a deep sense of privilege at coming to the centre of everything, in the suffering, and now glorified, Son of Man; our Saviour, our Lord – and our supreme tutor in the life of the kingdom. To face the *thlipsis* of the New Testament is to be identified with him, and he with us.

A Question Of Arithmetic

Let this chapter close with the story of Charles Simeon, Anglican vicar of Holy Trinity Church in Cambridge from 1782 until his death in 1836 – an amazing total of fifty-four of the most influential years of ministry ever given in England.

His biblical stance was deeply resented at the beginning, and this persisted for years, until the godly patience of his bearing turned the tide. In a conversation with a Mr Gurney he once related:

> Many years ago, when I was an object of much contempt and derision in this university, I strolled forth one day, buffeted and afflicted, with my little Testament in my hand. I prayed earnestly to my God, that he would comfort me with some cordial from his Word, and that, on opening the Book, I might find some text which should sustain me. The first text which caught my eye was this: *They found a man of Cyrene, Simon by name; him they compelled to carry his cross.* You know Simon is the same name as Simeon. What a world of instruction was here – what a blessed hint for my encouragement! To have the cross laid upon me, that I might bear it after Jesus – what a privilege! It was enough. Now I could leap and sing for joy as one whom Jesus was honouring with a participation in his sufferings.

The Stone That Became A Mountain

Hast thou no scar? No hidden scar on foot, or side,
or hand?
I hear thee sung as mighty in the land,
I hear them hail thy bright ascendant star,
Hast thou no scar?

Hast thou no wound? Yet I was wounded by the
archers, spent,
Leaned me against a tree to die; and rent
By ravening wolves that compassed me,
I swooned;
Hast thou no wound?

No wound, no scar?
Yet, as the Master shall the servant be,
and pierced are the feet that follow Me;
But thine are whole; can he have followed far
who hath no wound, no scar?

   (From *Streams in the Desert*, Amy Carmichael)

Part Four

Living the Kingdom

The men who wrote the Epistles stress that we who are Christians are living in two ages at once. We experience the trials, temptations, and problems of this present age, even though we have tasted the powers of the coming age. God is king right now, but He doesn't always 'flex His kingly muscles'. Rather than totally wiping out sin and its results, He gives Christians a mere taste or 'down payment' of what the kingdom in its fullness will be like.

(Joni Eareckson and Steve Estes, *A Step Further*, Marshall Pickering)

10

The World Is Waiting For You

'A man of noble birth went to a distant country to have himself appointed king and then to return. So he called ten of his servants and gave them ten minas. "Put this money to work," he said, "until I come back."' (Luke 19:12-13)

One of the greatest evangelists who ever lived was Kate Booth, daughter of the founder of the Salvation Army. She was already speaking to large crowds when she was fifteen. Her experiences when she visited France and ministered in the dives of Paris earned her the nickname of 'La Maréchale' ('The Marshall'). In later life, when people flocked to hear her, it was asked, 'Why do you travel so far to come to her meetings?' 'Because', came the answer, 'she makes Jesus more real than any speaker we have ever heard.' General Booth himself would testify of his gifted young daughter, 'She is my Blücher. When all else fails, put on Katie!'

But the sense of calling was being instilled into the Maréchale from her very earliest days. When she was four, her mother would tuck her into bed with the words, 'Now, Katie, you are not here in this world for yourself. You are here for God and for others. The world is waiting for you.'

They were great words to send a little girl to bed with! As she grew up, Kate Booth would say to herself, 'Mother says the world is waiting for me.'

Through her Spirit-filled speaking, people obeyed the summons to follow Christ, by the tens of thousand.

The nineteenth chapter of Luke's Gospel presents us with a parable on the wonderful privilege – and frightening responsibility – of being Christ's earthly representative before an entire world.

Jesus is about to take his final leave of Jericho, with its green palms and tall cypress trees. Ahead of him lies the 15-mile dusty road that will take him to Bethany and on to Jerusalem, where he will die for the sins of the world. Already, among his disciples and other Passover pilgrims about to take the same road, expectations are building up. 'This is going to be no ordinary Passover,' many were thinking. Would it provide Jesus with the opportunity to claim his kingdom and end the Roman tyranny at one stroke?

Close at hand is Zacchaeus, the newest recruit for the kingdom of God. Why, as chief tax collector, he had been part of the hated imperial system!

Was all of that about to be swept away? Faces are turned towards Jesus, alight with eager interest:

He went on to tell them a parable, because he was near Jerusalem and the people thought that the kingdom of God was going to appear at once (Luke 19:11).

Jesus was going to correct the false impression. The story was simple enough. A top person takes a long journey, in order to receive a kingdom for himself – leaving his trustees to work and trade on his behalf until his return.

What Luke 19 doesn't tell us – but what we learn from the Jewish historian Josephus – is that the parable was a story within a story. For every bystander knew that only a matter of years earlier, King Herod had received his kingdom by making the long journey to Rome, where the title 'King of the Jews' was given him. When he died in 4 BC, his kingdom was divided between his three sons – all of whom in their turn were required to travel to Rome to receive their share, their own kingdom.

It was the eldest son, Herod Archelaus, whose journey to claim his kingdom – that of Judea – was bitterly opposed by the locals, who said (in the words of Luke 19:14), 'We don't want this man to be our king.' In point of fact, Archelaus returned successfully from Rome, although he was never actually given the title of 'King'.

Jesus' words, then, were full of historical echoes. Listeners would immediately have identified the travelling nobleman with Archelaus. There would also have been a parallel between Christ himself and

Archelaus – not in the morality of their kingdoms, but in the rebellion they invited.

A different kind of kingdom was about to be claimed by Jesus through his death in Jerusalem, and it would be resisted. The time would come when he would visibly depart, leaving his representatives to carry out the business of the kingdom in his name and on his behalf. At the end of the age he will return – with rewards for those trustees who have been faithful, but in judgment upon his enemies.

'The world is waiting for you.' The call is for an investment, in the kingdom of God, of our energies and potential – equivalent to the one pound or mina of Greek currency. The whole parable is couched in unashamedly commercial terms.

We are here for a long stay

'A distant country until I come back' – the implication is that the king's absence would be prolonged, and that his trustees were committed to an extensive programme.

Some of us have always reckoned on this. The old Anglican Prayer Book, in one of its fascinating tables of festivals, generously makes provision for establishing the date of Easter as far ahead as AD 8500. With such long-range faith did our forebears plan for the future!

But let's think commercially. On most fronts, 'short-termism' commands little respect. Business people, investigating possible projects, will ask, 'Is this an operational issue?' By this they mean, 'Is this a project simply for today? A one-off?' Alternatively they will say, 'Is this a tactical project?' They are concerned to know if a short-term plan is being proposed; a temporary, a tactical manoeuvre. Or they may ask, thirdly, 'Is this strategic?' 'Is this the big one that commits us to a long-term programme?' The long term is the approved policy of most solid businesses – even if it costs a lot, to begin with.

This last is the emphasis of Christ's parable. The kingdom was not about to sweep all before it, even though the great turning-point of the cross and resurrection was close at hand. Shortly there would follow the visible departure of the King, with an extensive mission meanwhile entrusted to his representatives.

We cannot be in the work of the kingdom and entertain the idea of a quick flutter, or the equivalent of a fluke business killing. There will be no short-cuts. As we have seen earlier, Jesus overcame every temptation to obtain his kingdom the easy way. By his example he set the norm for generations ahead. Stephen Neill writes:

> Throughout the centuries, the Church of Christ has survived only because there has been within it a sufficient number of men and women who were willing, if need arose, cheerfully to die for him (*Christian Faith Today*, Pelican).

And if not to die, to struggle and persist in the long battle against unbelief and injustice.

129

The two Wesley brothers, John and Charles, provided us with a model over two centuries ago. 'We are going to change the course of history,' they resolved, as their sermons (40,000 of them) and their hymns (7,000 of them) steadily diverted England from the revolutionary violence that would engulf France across the Channel.

In the course of riding the equivalent of ten times round the world, John Wesley wrote:

> I earnestly exhorted those who believed, to beware of two opposite extremes – the one, thinking, while they were in light and joy, that the work was ended, when it was but just begun; the other, thinking, when they were in heaviness, that it was not begun, because they found it was not ended (*Journals*, 19 November 1739).

Three years later Wesley observed, 'O let none think his labour of love is lost because the fruit does not immediately appear!' The last letter he ever wrote was one of encouragement to William Wilberforce, whose fight in Parliament against the injustice of the slave trade lasted a long twenty years. Written on 24 February 1791, six days before his own death, Wesley's words should challenge any who are tempted to think that the combating of social evil is no part of Christ's mission on earth:

> Unless God has raised you up for this very thing, you will be worn out by the opposition of men and devils; but if God is with you who can be against

you? O be not weary in well-doing. Go on, in the name of God and in the power of his might till even American slavery, the vilest that ever saw the sun, shall vanish away before it.

Wesley's 'stay' was a long one! He was given fifty years as a vigorous trustee of the kingdom. At eighty-six years of age he was still hard at it when he wrote, 'I would fain do a little for the Lord before I drop into the dust' (*Journals*, 1790, 26 March 1790).

We're here to produce results

Again, let us stay with the language of commerce. 'Put this money to work [literally "trade"] until I come back.' The implication of Jesus' story is that the spreading of his kingdom is the biggest business going. It will never look like it, but when all else has gone, the kingdom of God will be the only thing in evidence. It is thus the only cause worth the devotion of a lifetime.

Kate Booth, already referred to, was travelling through France when still a young woman. A man in the same train compartment recognized her and confided that he had seen her at work in Valence. And then, as though to demonstrate that he did his bit too, he added, 'I go to church every week.'

The Maréchale looked at him amazed.

'Is that all you do?' she asked. 'For a dying world? You go to church?' (*The Heavenly Witch* by Carolyn Scott, Hamish Hamilton)

The parable of Luke 19 is different from that of Matthew 25:14-30, in which stewards of different abilities are given varying large sums to trade with. In the Matthew parable, we are reminded of the different gifts that are entrusted to us to develop in the service of Christ. But in Luke 19, the sums dealt out are comparatively small (a mina was roughly three months' wages) – and they are all equal. The message to these listeners in Jericho was that every servant is given an equal and basic responsibility – to develop and use the one lifetime opportunity for the good of the kingdom.

In Jesus' mind, the world is like a great trading mart. Each steward has his or her own capacity for management. Might the stewards one day have the trusteeship of five, or even ten, cities? Well, let's see how they can first cope with the management of a single mina. Start small! In the words of Alexander Solzhenitsyn, 'Only one life is allotted us! One small, short life.'

There is no need to wait for the opportunity; it is there already, in front of us, if we are servants of Christ: we can begin at once! As I read the Scriptures, as I come with my friends to meet with God in the Christian fellowship, as I consider my circle of acquaintances, my assets and abilities, my money and my influence, I can ask myself, 'How can I please the King of my life, visibly absent in the present, but one day returning for an account of the overall return?'

It is a mental thing – the difference between being a consumer and being a contributor. Not all are meant to be pioneer missionaries, blazing evangelists or influential thinkers. Whatever the calling – philanthropic, political, domestic or financial – the members of the kingdom are not here for themselves. John Laing, whose name was internationally prominent in the building industry, made millions in his lifetime. But most of his fortune was ploughed into the interests of the kingdom of God. We would have to go further and say this of all of his fortune, for when he died in his ninety-ninth year, his net personal estate came out at £371!

John Laing had learnt the lesson decades back – that these assets were never his. His own modesty tied in with that of the servants in the parable. It was not a case of 'I made ten minas', but rather 'Sir, your mina has earned ten more!' It is only a small reminder, but it's there. It was never your mission, your college department, your organization. All you have is the trusteeship, and, if it is well exercised, the reward is greater trust still from God.

We must learn to adopt the mind-set of the kingdom when frustration and failure threaten to crush us. Christians placed in 'unrewarding' no-hope environments of work, family or Christian service, can rightly be comforted by the perception that God may be paying them a great compliment. Would he give such a situation to someone he could not trust?

The alternative is to be without the reward of knowing that we pleased him. Such was the disgrace of the third servant, who made no use at all of the assets entrusted to him. Perhaps he was a servant only in name, for his words hardly exhibit an attitude of trustful obedience (Luke 19:20). It seems that from the beginning he had no intention of producing any results for the king.

We're here to prepare for an audit

We are still in the language of the business house. Many boards of directors have audit committees, to measure their results and to ask, 'Is everything in order?' A day of accounting is built into their thinking.

Come back to those listeners in Jericho. For the majority of them, the impending journey of Jesus to Jerusalem represented the potential fulfilling of all their messianic hopes. They were dreaming of a Jewish political kingdom on earth that would obliterate every enemy. Christ's parable smashes the dream into fragments. A 'distant' journey is in prospect. When the King does ultimately return it will be in final judgment – to reward the faithful but to destroy those who had insisted to the end, 'We don't want this man to be our king.'

The third, unproductive, servant appears not to have been a true servant at all. He accuses the returning king of being hard and selfish. He seems to be in the story as a reminder to us that life in the kingdom of God is not a religion of impersonal 'good works' - of trying to please a hard taskmaster and so to earn our way into heaven. Rather we are in the realm of relationships, and service of the King

134

is the glad response of gratitude for all that he has done – and suffered – in claiming his kingdom.

The faithless servant is also present in the parable as an illustration of our Lord's punchline:

> 'I tell you that to everyone who has, more will be given, but as for the one who has nothing, even what he has will be taken away' (Luke 19:26).

It is not that, in God's service, the rich get richer and the poor, poorer; it is the principle that we see in daily life – that, where aptitudes and opportunities are concerned, you either use them or you lose them.

• Using is better than owning.

• Spending is better than hoarding.

• Trading is better than playing.

Could there be a better reward than knowing what God did with our lives, however humble or unseen the setting in which we were placed? It may be that part of the reward consists of people, people whom in one way or another we were enabled to serve during our short stay on planet Earth. It would be a wonderful thing to be identified before the King at the gates of heaven, when our turn comes: 'Lord, that's the person who introduced me to the Scriptures... that's the one who cared for me throughout my infirmity and illness... that's the one who campaigned for our freedom... who set up the youth camp... Lord, that's my fellowship group leader.'

It was a Japanese Christian leader, Toyohiko Kagawa, who once commented,

> I read in a Book that a man called Christ went about doing good. It is very disconcerting that I am so easily satisfied with just going about.

In a world that at times seems to be shaking itself to pieces, the great imperative – in the visible absence of the King – is the steady, day-by-day business of his kingdom. There is a world waiting out there.

11

Out In The Arena

> As servants of God we commend ourselves in every
> way ... in truthful speech and in the power of God;
> with weapons of righteousness in the right hand
> and in the left: through glory and dishonour, bad
> report and good report; genuine, yet regarded as
> impostors; known, yet regarded as unknown; dying,
> and yet we live on; beaten, and yet not killed;
> sorrowful, yet always rejoicing; poor, yet making
> many rich; having nothing, and yet possessing
> everything. (2 Corinthians 6:4, 7-10)

On more than one occasion I have sat as a guest
in the commentary box at the Wimbledon tennis
championships. It is a wonderful privilege. There you
are, elbow to elbow with the mighty, including usually
at least one ex-champion, watching superb tennis
from a brilliant viewing position. There's only one
disadvantage: you are not involved in what is going
on out there on court. No-one, but no-one, ever
applauds within the commentary box! No-one takes
sides and no-one can afford to get excited, beyond
the professional animation expected of a top

commentator. You are behind soundproof glass, hermetically sealed off from the crowd, the players and the immediacy of the drama taking place on the Centre Court. The crowd may have gone berserk as Rafter and Ivanisovic battled it out in the great final of 2001, but you within the glass were not personally committed.

Given the choice, nothing surely could ever fully compensate for the passivity of non-involvement! Certainly when a classic struggle is under way; even more so, when there are issues of life and death, heaven and hell, being fought over in the wider arena of God's world. I have seen something happen again and again in the lives of new believers in Christ; an entire world opens up to their interest and energies. It is a vista that they never dreamed of in the days of their narrow, this-life-only outlook.

You don't even have to travel for this to happen. My missionary father was once addressing a Christian meeting in Harrogate, North Yorkshire. Afterwards, two elderly women approached him. They were sisters.

'We didn't like to come up and introduce ourselves,' they admitted. 'In fact at the start of the meeting we said to each other, "We won't talk with him when this is over." But now we've heard you, we felt we must. You see,' they continued, 'you've been in our prayers for the last twenty-five years. You and every member of your family. Every day.'

The story then came out. The two sisters had seen my father's photograph in a missionary paper when he first left home for missionary service in East Africa. They put him on their prayer list. When he married there was an extra name to remember. Four children were duly born. Each was faithfully prayed for daily. When the family finally returned to England the prayers never ceased.

These two praying women had never left their country. But by their prayers they were crossing oceans, defying international boundaries and entering numerous countries, some of which were closed to Christian missions. They had, not a prayer list, but a prayer room. On its walls were news clippings, extracts from missionary magazines – and scores of photographs of people for whom they were praying daily but had never met. Our family was among them.

Nothing is impossible to such people. It may be asked, 'Who are the influential, the key-workers in the kingdom of God?' At the end of time the answer will surely be seen to lie in the two intercessors of Harrogate and their like, all over the world. They occupy the centre of the arena.

To be accurate, there is more than one arena making demands upon the prayers and priorities of God's people. These spheres of activity seem to confront us in pairs. To neglect one sphere at the expense of another is to become lopsided in our effectiveness. In some cases we can become extremists. All our lives we must wrestle with these tensions that lie at the heart of kingdom life. They are basic to the Bible's teaching.

The private and universal

These two spheres are not at war with each other, of course. Common to them both is the New Testament assertion that 'Jesus is Lord'.

It begins with a personal conviction, expressed by an individual in response to the sacrifice for sin made by Jesus Christ. Without that, there is no mainspring, no forgiveness, new birth or Holy Spirit, no life at all.

Christ confronts an individual, much as the Roman senator Popillius intercepted Antiochus Epiphanes in 186 BC (see chapter 1). Notwithstanding the occasion – a Christian meeting, a discussion or the reading of a book – a circle is drawn around us. 'Answer me', commands the Son of Man, 'before you leave this place!' We bow before the incoming authority of a kingdom bigger than anything we have ever known. Christ becomes Lord of our lives; of our ethics, work, relationships and future plans, even of our very bedrooms.

But it cannot stop at the private realm. If it could, we are safe in saying that Christianity's foray into Europe wouldn't have got beyond Antioch. Here was a new way of looking at life altogether. A man had died for the sins of the world. He had been raised, and was now ascended far above all rule and authority, power and dominion (Ephesians 1:21). Had the early Christians been content to worship Jesus as an optional extra – in addition to their state obligations to Caesar – there would have been no problem for them.

It was their refusal to worship God and Caesar that marked them out for persecution. 'Jesus is Lord' was their creed. This meant that nobody else could be Lord, and all other gods were false. If this conviction is unpopular today, it is nothing new. For many in the Roman empire it meant death.

'Why can't there be a fusion, a synthesis of traditions?' it is asked today. Our answer should be quite firm: 'It's already been done in one man!' Could there be anyone bigger than Christ as a unifier of the human race?

> For God was pleased to have all his fulness dwell in him, and through him to reconcile to himself all things, whether things on earth or things in heaven, by making peace through his blood, shed on the cross (Col. 1:19-20).

A sermon had been preached in our church, on Christ as 'the way, the truth and the life' (John 14:6). The words were still ringing in our ears: 'No-one comes to the Father, except through me.' Afterwards a man of another religion stopped by me on his way out:

'I agree with those words', he said smilingly. 'They were true for that time. But since then there have come fresh manifestations of God, further representatives.'

We held a little discussion while worshippers walked out past us. Three points occurred to me:

• What Christ did on the cross, he did for ever. The New Testament is full of references to his 'once-for-all' sacrifice, accomplished 'at the end of time', 'for ever' (e.g. Hebrews 7:20-28; 9:26-28; 1 Peter 1:20).

• No-one could ever improve on Christ. Morally and in every way, he simply stands alone (1 Peter 2:21-25).

• Jesus warned us not to believe those who would come, after his time, claiming to be Christ. He emphasized that the only time he will reappear will be at the close of the age, when his coming will be public, unannounced and sudden – and in final judgment (Matthew 24:23-51). He is unique and universal; there can never be another!

But the very universality of his kingdom means that we are to bear witness to his rule as it touches every part of public life, political, social, educational, medical or cultural.

At first sight, it may not have looked that way in the New Testament church. Where were the protest marches, the sit-ins? After all, there were sixty million slaves in the Roman empire; why didn't the apostles urge them to throw off their shackles and defy the system? The answer is that if the apostles had gone down that road, they would have reduced Christ to the stature of a mere Spartacus or Karl Marx. They did something more radical altogether. Within their own ranks began a movement of subversion. The Christians chose, among themselves, to ignore the system and treat the divisions between slave and master as though they didn't exist at all.

The New Testament letter to Philemon is devoted entirely to this issue.

The apostle Paul – himself in prison – urges the Christian slave-owner Philemon to receive back his newly converted runaway slave 'no longer as a slave, but better than a slave, as a dear brother' (Philemon 16). Paul was prepared, if necessary, to offset Philemon's financial loss in setting his slave free.

'Be among the first,' was Paul's message to Philemon. Elsewhere he wrote, 'There is neither Jew nor Greek, slave nor free, male nor female, for you are all one in Christ Jesus' (Galatians 3:28).

Here in the letter to Philemon lay a principle that was to become a policy. It represented a time bomb of truth, ticking away in the heart of Rome. The time would come when Christ's kingdom would stand over the grave of the once mighty empire. The time would come when William Wilberforce – fired by his evangelical convictions – would engage in a forty-year campaign with his friends, to force his famous Bill through the British parliament, outlawing the slave trade for ever. The time would come when missionaries, on the east and west coasts of Africa, would do battle with the slave-traders, whether Arab or American.

When the Christian convictions of the private realm are brought to bear upon the public and universal domain, the result has been described as 'the stabilizing of society without sterilizing it'. Unless the attempt is made, we cannot be said to be fully in the arena. But here are two further spheres of service that we have to hold in tension.

The verbal and the visible

It has been said that, while there are those who have a vision for the King but not for the kingdom, there are others who have a vision for the kingdom but not for the King. Another way of expressing the tension is by setting salvation against service, the preachers and evangelists against the activists and relief-workers. At times the irritation between the two groups has become pronounced.

The tension is greatly eased when we take our eyes off ourselves and our activities, and ask ourselves what God has done in the gospel, and what he is doing in our world today.

Jesus Christ, God's Son, is Master of the world! He has fought and beaten down King Death, and at the cross he has overcome the principalities and unseen powers. He has brought into being his redeemed church, and poured upon it the gift of his empowering Spirit. A new situation confronts an unbelieving world. The church is here, and to it has been entrusted the task of living and proclaiming the kingdom. Provided it is doing its job, and provided Christ is at the centre of its life (or it is no true church), then we can expect the usurping powers and authorities to be extremely uncomfortable! Here is a new society that stands for truth, peace and justice. Further, it is heralding a future which leaves no room for the old order. The words proclaimed by this new community are powerful words – powerful enough to challenge evil and to bring down strongholds! In such a situation it is pathetic even to think of opposing word and action against each other. A Christ-centred movement is going to be alive in its preaching, its praise, its spill-over into society.

Our family once received a letter from a Christian leader in the Sudan:

'It is wonderful to be here. The gospel is powerful, and it is expected to be powerful.'

The church in Thailand came into being, initially, largely through the work being done by the followers of Christ among its leprosy sufferers. In the history of the world there has been scarcely a group found anywhere with the willingness to go near those afflicted with leprosy. It is to the everlasting credit of Jesus Christ that in every age there were men and women who were glad, for his sake, to tend to the leprosy patients and share in the Holy Communion with them.

The verbal and the visible always belonged together in the ministry of Jesus, and so it must be in every era. It is only when the King himself is left out of the reckoning that any programme – of word or action – can be expected to falter. The evangelical reformer of the nineteenth century, the Earl of Shaftesbury, once declared, 'Education, without instruction in moral and spiritual principles, will merely produce a race of clever devils.' But there is a third area in which two aspects of life in God's kingdom at times ride uneasily with each other.

The 'already' and the 'not yet'

A smiling East African Asian came up to me at the end of one of our services at All Souls Church. I had been preaching on the final completion of the kingdom of God, on the return of Christ and the life of heaven.

'I want it now!' he bubbled.

As I smiled back I could only agree. We then rallied each other's spirits with the reminder that the tensions of living as Christians in central London were entirely biblical tensions. For both of us the kingdom of God had become a thrilling reality through its arrival in the person of Jesus. It had come! But it was not yet completed. The in-between time of temptations, trials – and tantalizing 'fore-tastes' of the future glory – can be hard to endure. Yet we can live with these tensions once we understand them.

• It's the tension of having started the race without yet completing it.

• It's the tension of having been saved from sin's penalty but not from its presence.

• It's the tension of having been 'raised with

Christ' in the resurrection life, but still awaiting a body free from pain and sickness.

- It's the tension of living under the reign of Jesus in a world that has not yet acknowledged his rule.

That final, wonderful day has 'not yet' come, and we can hardly wait for its arrival!

Many are the times in Christian experience when people have become tired of waiting and battling, and have given in, either to negative defeatism or empty triumphalism, and both are alternative forms of despair.

The defeatist (who tends to take a loose view of Scripture) cannot believe in a future glory and consummation, and so tries to establish the kingdom entirely in the here and now. 'This is it: there's nothing more.' At its most extreme, it has taken the form of the Marxist utopian dream of a kingdom achievable here on earth.

The triumphalist (who is likely to have started from a position of believing the Bible) falls into two traps: first that of underestimating the wonder of Calvary, Easter and Pentecost – and of Christian conversion; and secondly that of exaggerating what is promised to us this side of heaven. Experience takes over from the Bible. Heaven itself, as a future confidence, is lost sight of, in the attempt to make it all happen in the here and now – health, peace, prosperity, and the banishment of tears and trials.

The end of both positions, defeatism and triumphalism, lies in the direction of ultimate disillusionment, for both are trying in their own way to create heaven in the immediate present. And, as Lesslie Newbigin has written,

> 'The project of bringing heaven down to earth always results in bringing hell up from below' (*Foolishness to the Greeks*, SPCK).

It was the extremism of the false teachers at Corinth that caused the apostle Paul his greatest heartaches. His words are stabbed with irony, but they could have been written today:

> Already you have all you want! Already you have become rich! You have become kings – and that without us! ... We are fools for Christ, but you are so wise in Christ! We are weak, but you are strong! You are honoured, we are dishonoured! To this very hour we go hungry and thirsty, we are in rags, we are brutally treated, we are homeless (1 Corinthians 4:8, 10-11).

We may marvel at the staying power of Christians like Paul of Tarsus, John Wesley and Kate Booth. They could stay out in the arena of witness and never-ending service for decades on end, outfacing and even outliving the representatives of another kingdom in a terrifyingly dark world. They could only do so because they had their framework of thought well-established. And they kept their gaze steadily upon the City not made with hands, that spoke of a future glory that will one day fill the earth 'as the waters cover the sea'.

To that glory we now come in our final chapter.

12

The Glory Of The Kingdom

He who was seated on the throne said, 'I am making
everything new!' (Revelation 21:5)

It falls to certain individuals to be credited with
being among the most powerful people in the world.
There was one such, who was born in AD 51. By the
time he was thirty, he was *it*. He inherited an empire
whose borders were the Euphrates, the Danube, the
Rhine, the Atlantic and the northern edge of the
African desert. He needed no warships on the
Mediterranean, because the Mediterranean was one
vast Roman lake. The Roman imperial eagle was in
evidence everywhere – by the cataracts of the Nile,
on the shores of Boulogne, even on the hills above
Carlisle.

There were sixty million slaves in the empire that
was governed by this one powerful individual, Titus
Flavius Domitian. By the time he was in his forties,
his behaviour had become so intolerable, even to
the pagans of his time, that conspiracies were hatched
for his overthrow, the last one being successful in

AD 96, when he was assassinated at the age of forty-five.

The book of Revelation was written around the year AD 95 – when Domitian had one more year to live. To be a declared Christian at that time was to be living on a permanent knife-edge – living, as you were, under the rule of a tyrant who demanded to be worshipped. Even to be found in possession of a document such as the Apocalypse would guarantee you a one-way ticket to the arena of the Colosseum.

To read the book of Revelation is to expose yourself to the sheer strength and momentum of the New Testament church, whose calling it was to show the world for all time how we outlive and outlast tyrannies. Just as Daniel and his friends survived the Babylonian tyranny through the vision of the stone that became a mountain, so did the believers of Domitian's reign triumph against all the odds, with their grasp of the victory of God in Jesus Christ.

Basically, it has been the same vision all along the line. The ladder of Jacob's dream, the child of Isaiah's prophecy, the stone of Daniel's vision, the writing on the wall, the voice at Christ's baptism, the spectacle of the transfiguration, the unveiling of heaven shared equally by the dying Stephen and the exiled John ... we are inheritors of these glimpses of the kingdom in its thrilling future consummation. If we lose sight of that, then with the rest of the world we shall lurch on, baffled by every twist and turn of this chaotic age.

Our vision of the future makes sense of the present

'Aim at heaven,' wrote C. S. Lewis, 'and you will get "earth" thrown in as well. Aim at earth, and you will get neither.'

It is a strange paradox, but John, the writer of the book of Revelation, would have agreed. While Domitian – or any other Caesar – was on the imperial throne, the likelihood was that the average Christian believer within the Roman empire would have been unnerved by the sheer power of what the Faith was up against – but for the fact that heaven was opened in this remarkable and prophetic tract for the times. Above and around the earthly kingdom of Rome was another kingdom, centred in a throne which, whatever the provocation on earth, was permanently occupied and eternally unshakeable. Just to glimpse that throne, and the victory of Christ the Lamb, is to gain a new perspective on everything. And knowing the future helps!

1. *It makes sense of our present turbulence.* 'There was no longer any sea,' writes the apostle John in Revelation 21:1. In more than one instance 'the sea' is taken, biblically, to symbolize the instability of struggling heathen nations and peoples (Isaiah 17:12; Revelation 17:15). But in the new heaven and new earth of the future, the upheavals and revolutions, the power politics and tidal waves of human displacement will be replaced by a great calm, under a new order. Just to know this helps believers of

every generation to live with the turbulences of the present, and even to understand them.

2. *It makes sense of the church's frustrations.* The twenty-first chapter of Revelation presents the Christian church in a waiting situation, as a bride preparing for the wedding feast, for the arrival of Christ the Bridegroom. That is our ultimate destiny. Meanwhile the going is extremely rough. Is there a single place on earth where it is easy? But to be aware of the loud voice from the throne itself, with its assurance that the day is approaching when our fellowship with God will be direct and immediate, and that the frustrations of this waiting period will be over (Revelation 21:3) – why, to know what the future holds is to give us an extra gear!

3. *It makes sense of the problem of pain.* Pain will not be for ever. The Revelation is given to us to pull back a tiny corner of the curtain and to say, 'Look beyond!'

> He will wipe every tear from their eyes. There will be no more death or mourning or crying or pain, for the old order of things has passed away (Revelation 21:4).

Again, as we have seen elsewhere in Scripture, we are confronted by the 'tense of the prophetic past' – so certain will be the fulfilment! For those who are buffeted by hardships and handicaps, a proper view of the future puts these troubles in the context of a bigger, eternal scenario in which the afflictions will be seen as 'light and momentary' (2 Corinthians 4:17). They are not for ever, and to know this is a help.

4. *It makes sense of our tangled history.* From the throne (Revelation 21:5-6) comes the assurance that everything is to be remade in the new order; that God, as the Alpha and Omega, stands astride our existence. He sees the end from the beginning, as we cannot.

Once more I like the tense of the prophetic past (21:6): 'It is done.' But what is done? The answer can only be in terms of the fulfilment and consummation of God's kingly rule. It is stated as though it has already happened. There is a future glory coming.

5. *It makes sense of our unfulfilled hopes.* Some of the things we thirst to achieve will never be attained in this life. So often, however, our earthly strivings are only symptomatic of the altogether deeper thirst for significance, for a relationship with God, promised to the one 'who overcomes', and it is this thirst that will be met 'from the spring of the water of life' (21:6-7). There will be no frustration in the future order.

6. *It makes sense of the challenge of evil.* Our papers and TV are full of it – complaints that terrible acts have taken place and the perpetrators have been allowed to 'walk away', freed often on some legal technicality. But the Bible speaks of a higher court, and of perfect justice. The vile, the immoral and the murderers will not get away with it (21:8). Judgment is coming – as a logical necessity.

When we read – back in Revelation 17 – of the apparent triumph of evil, incarnated in a figure that is identified with the wicked city of Babylon, we are reminded of similar incarnations today that laugh in our face. To quote Solzhenitsyn:

> It has already come to pass that the demon of evil, like a whirlwind, triumphantly circles all five continents of the earth.

We would find it very hard to handle this phenomenon of evil, but for the timeless assurance that fortified the Christians in the terrible days of Domitian. The whole edifice of evil is going to go up in smoke. The reaction of heaven and its citizens will be unanimous and heartfelt:

> 'Hallelujah!
> The smoke from her goes up for ever
> and ever.'   (Revelation 19:3)

To read the last pages of the Bible is to turn you into an indomitable optimist! Our view of the future makes sense of the present. But there is more to say.

Our vision of the centre gives shape to the whole
The centre? By that we mean the throne of God, the focus of all power (Revelation 21:3, 5). Early in the Apocalypse we are presented with the vision of the throne, as though to fortify the reader for some

of the alarming descriptions of 'what must soon take place'.

The plagues, the catastrophes, deceptions, persecutions, conflicts and endless pressures on the saints – why, it seems that Satan and his allies are active everywhere! Where is God, all this time? The reassuring answer is that God never leaves the throne. The centre remains intact throughout.

In my little book *The Lamb Wins* (Christian Focus) I try to give a 'birds'-eye view' of the book of Revelation, and make the point that the events portrayed to us are patterns of what we are to expect during the entire period between Christ's first and second comings. When and wherever they take place, the believer is not to be shocked. It is as we stay close to the throne – escorted there in prayer every day by Christ our mediator – that we can acquire a heavenly perspective on what is taking place in our world.

The call goes out world-wide at times of great stress, for believing people to come back to the Bible and to rediscover prayer. As the Argentinian evangelist Luís Palau once said at a press conference, 'It's back to the Bible, or it's back to the jungle!' It is as we engage in these two great disciplines – prayer and the Bible – that we maintain that vital firm contact with our HQ! Once we lose that contact, and we are at the mercy of every deceptive power and psychic epidemic rampaging our world today.

Our view of the throne at the centre enables us to hold on to reality! It helps us to see the direction and shape of our human affairs within the purposes of God's kingdom and to remain unshaken.

At one point in the historic Battle of Waterloo in 1815, Napoleon attempted to set up a diversion, and so to draw precious troops away from Wellington's centre. But the Iron Duke was not to be tempted. From his vantage-point he had a commanding view of the entire battlefield, and was able to recognize his opponent's tactics. Even when pressed by his generals to release some troops, Wellington replied coldly, 'I do not intend to run about like a wet hen.' His centre stayed unbroken.

At times we shall know ourselves to be in the thick of battle, spiritually, mentally, philosophically. Our vision of the centre, where God rules, gives us a vantage-point that cannot be found anywhere else. Here is the secret of a world-view that has shape to it; here is the secret of staying intact. But there is yet another.

Our vision of the triumph adds strength to the task

Our spirits lift as we come to the grand finale of the Bible, and sense that we are riding into history alongside the Rider on the white horse (Revelation 19:11-16). But now it is history seen through God's eyes, as the outward layers of the world's storyline are peeled away – the struggles, the rise and fall of its great kingdoms; here we are penetrating to the inner plot, the theme behind the headlines.

It is not an obscure secret, open only to certain select initiates. It is an open secret, available to shepherds and kings alike, to illiterate fishermen as well as to eggheads like Saul of Tarsus.

It is the story of love and reconciliation on the part of the Creator; offered freely, yet through bloody sacrifice, to a race of rebels fed on a trash-can of lies. It is the story of how the kingdoms of this world become the kingdom of the Lord and of his Christ. It is the story in which a Roman cross of execution and an empty grave figure centrally. It is the story of an ever-growing family of believers, a crowd that no-one can number – the biggest family of faith that has ever been seen on earth. Every day some 80,000 new members are joined, through the new birth, to its ranks. Every week some 1,600 new congregations come into being.

It is the story that – despite its catalogue of martyrdoms and sufferings – ends in overwhelming victory, and the complete ascendency of Christ, the bright Morning Star (Revelation 22:16).

Some may ask, 'Is membership of the kingdom worth all the cost?' Mention has already been made of the Iranian Christian martyr, Mehdi Dibaj. Let him provide us with a modern answer, from his final testament, addressed to his jailors and ultimately finding its way into *The Times* of 18 January 1994:

> He is our Saviour and He is the Son of God. To know Him means to know eternal life. I, a useless sinner, have believed in His beloved person and all

his words and miracles recorded in the gospel, and I have committed my life into His hands. Life for me is an opportunity to serve Him, and death is a better opportunity to be with Christ. Therefore I am not only satisfied to be in prison for the honour of His Holy Name, but am ready to give my life for the sake of Jesus my Lord and enter His kingdom sooner, the place where the elect of God enter everlasting life, but the wicked to eternal damnation.

May the shadow of God's kindness and His hand of blessing and healing be upon you and remain for ever. Amen.

With respect,

Your Christian Prisoner,

Mehdi Dibaj

These closing words of a ringing Christian testimony made their own profound impression on *The Times* columnist, Bernard Levin, self-confessedly not a Christian, but moved to the point of giving his entire column over to Mehdi's complete text. The words have a New Testament ring about them and are shot through with the glory of the kingdom.

It is the vision of 'the city with foundations', the 'better country' (Hebrews 11:8-16) that imparts courage, strength and a holy joy even in the hardest of this earth's predicaments.

Four cautions, and then we are through:

• Don't join the *myopics* – the short-sighted ones! If three-score years and ten form your boundary, then you are living an unbelievably narrow life.

There is another land – a whole world – of discovery and adventure, if you will only let Abraham, Moses and Daniel, Paul and Stephen, Janani Luwum and Mehdi Dibaj tutor your vision; to take in, and be energized by, the kingdom that dominated their horizon.

• Don't join the *romantics*. We must learn from the past, but we cannot live in the past. The romantic is all too often bedevilled by dreams of past glories, and reduced to wistful ineffectiveness by self-authenticating 'prophecies' of a revival that is just round the corner. We are the scriptwriters for today, in the life of the kingdom.

• Don't join the *cynics*. The cynic is equally ineffective in the belief that nothing in this world can change! A vigorous prayer life, inspired by the reading of the Bible and the Christian fellowship, is the answer to the mind-set of the cynic. The shock wave of Easter and the empty tomb will still be advancing when every modern rival movement has exhausted itself.

• Don't join the *hysterics*. There is a fine dividing line in society between the prophetic and the hysteric elements. We shouldn't be too ready to rush after every new phenomenon on the Christian scene, to believe every Christian book, to attend every Christian conference! The truth of the Bible is our touchstone, and the presence of a small circle of loving Christian people around us is our stability.

Another land is beckoning us all the time. Lose sight of it, and we will eventually be taken captive by one or other of the false kingdom views being peddled today. We began with Daniel and the stone that became a mountain. Let us end with an early twentieth century hymn, adapted and expanded for the twenty-first. It was first sung in our church in connection with the death of Diana, Princess of Wales in September 1997:

> I vow to you, my Saviour, all earthly things above,
> Entire and whole and perfect, the service of my love;
> The love that asks no questions, the love that stands the test,
> That lays upon his altar the dearest and the best;
> The love that never falters, the love that knows the price,
> The love that stands indebted before your sacrifice.
>
> And there's a royal country I've heard of long ago,
> It speaks of grace and heaven, a place that all may know;
> We may not count her armies, we may not see her King;
> Her emblem on a hilltop, the Cross of suffering,
> And soul by soul and silently, her citizens increase,
> Her ways are ways of gentleness and all her paths are peace.
>
> O tell me of the Kingdom that stands the test of time,
> O lead me to its gateway, and speak the word sublime
> That tells me I'm forgiven, my name is in the Book,
> The Cross of Jesus holds me, as heav'nward I look;

Baptised into a living hope, I'll walk the path that's new;
And the prize of God in Jesus for ever I'll pursue.

So light the fire within me, and let me fan the flame,
And fill me with the Spirit, that I may bear your Name;
In season and in hardship, to run my given race,
O keep me ever-burning until I see your face.
I vow to you, my Saviour, that where your feet have trod,
I'll serve and follow faithfully, my Master and my God!

After Sir Cecil Spring-Rise, revised and expanded, R.T.Bewes
Tune: Thaxted, Gustav Holst, 1874-1934
© Jubilate Hymns 1997

Study Guide for Groups

Part One: Expecting the kingdom

Are you in a study fellowship or house group, or a student meeting? These first two Bible studies relate to Part One of this book.

Study 1

Try **Isaiah 9:2-7** to begin with. After praying for God's help in understanding the passage, read the sentences in the passage and then discuss them. The following questions may help to stimulate the group.

1. What two main themes dominate verses 2 and 3 of Isaiah 9? How do these themes contrast with the closing verses of Isaiah 8:19-22?

2. Isaiah 9:4 refers to a favourite theme of the Jews, the defeat of the Midianites by Gideon. What was significant about that victory? For a cross-reference, see Judges 7 (verses 2 and 7 will give extra clues). Isaiah 9:4 is evidently addressed to the coming Deliverer. Why this allusion to Judges 7?

3. Come now to verses 6 and 7. From these words, try and describe the attributes of the coming Child.

4. How far do these attributes tie in with the four main characteristics of the kingdom of God (see page 27)?

5. Take the four great titles of the second half of verse 6. In what practical ways have any of them applied in the experience of members of the group?

6. Looking back to verse 2, what is 'the tense of the prophetic past' (see page 29)? What is its significance? What is its encouragement?

7. What is the dominant thought that comes across to the group from the passage as a whole? How would you apply the passage to current situations?

Study 2

Luke 1:46-55 provides a rewarding study. Two women, related to each other, have met: Elizabeth, the mother-to-be of John the Baptist, and Mary, who is expecting the birth of Jesus. This passage features Mary's words of praise, and gives us some powerful insights into the nature of Christ and the kingdom. These questions may stimulate your discussion.

1. Where do you read about 'tumbling kingdoms' in this passage? Why do they fall? The answer lies in the passage.

2. What do we learn here about (a) Mary's sense of privilege, and (b) her humility?

3. What can you discover from the passage about the universality, permanence and justice of God's kingdom?

4. Mary describes here the overturned values that God's rule introduces. Try to list them and discuss places and situations where they are being applied today.

5. 'Mighty deeds' (verse 51). How would you describe these deeds? How do they tie in with the character of God, described in these verses?

6. Begin to think of parts of the world where the kingdom of God is being severely contested, and engage in prayer for people involved who are known to you.

Part Two: Understanding the kingdom

With Part Two of this book as a background, we turn now to two passages relating to the nature of God's kingdom.

Study 3

Matthew 13:1-23 brings us to Jesus' parable of the sower. After praying for guidance in understanding, read the passage, and consider the following questions:

1. Here is a 'snapshot' of the kingdom of heaven. In the fate of the seed and the variety of the harvest, what is Jesus trying to say?

2. Why is the kingdom of heaven not uniformly successful on all fronts? Try to analyse what was going on as the seed fell. Describe in today's terms the four kinds of soil.

3. Look at verses 10-17. Talk about the sifting effect that the parables had on Jesus' listeners. What does this tell us about our own communication of the Christian good news? What should be the attitude of the believer in answering the questions of others?

4. In a world where quick results are seen to be desirable, what lessons can be learnt from this parable?

5. What is the answer to the charge of fatalism in this passage? Are certain hearts irrevocably hard? Turn this over in the light of verse 9, and compare Luke 8:18.

6. There is only one Sower, it seems. What part is to be played by the members of the kingdom?

7. What, in Christian terms today, is a good crop?

Study 4

John 3:1-16 introduces us to the Pharisee
Nicodemus, in his private interview with Jesus. From
it we can learn important truths about understanding
and entering the kingdom of God. The following
questions can be used to stimulate your discussions.

1. We may take Nicodemus' approach to Jesus as
sincere. If, like others, he was longing for the liberation
of Israel – and hoped that Jesus might be God's
instrument – what was his first surprise? What is the
only kingdom that matters? What makes a person a
member of it?

2. 'Born again'... 'born of the Spirit' (verses 3-8).
Nicodemus, as 'Israel's teacher' (verse 10), ought to
have known what Jesus was speaking about. Why?
(Compare Ezekiel 36:25-27; 37:9)

3. 'Water' (cleansing/forgiveness), 'Spirit' – how do
these wonderful gospel gifts tie in with the early
Christian preaching? (Compare Acts 2:38)

4. Talk together about the difficulty that people have
always had in understanding the spiritual and inward
principles of the kingdom, as against the earthly and
outward. How far has this been your experience?

5. What is the vital significance of verses 14 and 15?
(See Numbers 21:5-9)

6. John's comment is that this is universal truth (verse 16). How far do you accept that this is so?

Part Three: Heralding the kingdom

Here now are two studies from Psalms and Revelation, for which Part Three of this book forms the background material.

Study 5

Psalm 2 is one of the 'kingly', messianic psalms. This 'coronation psalm' is asking the question that everyone asks at a change-over of leadership, or when society seems to be wobbling out of control: 'Whatever is happening to our world?' Some questions on this passage:

1. In verses 1-3, can you analyse the basic attitudes adopted by the world's secular authorities? How general are these attitudes, and why are they adopted?

2. Try to think through the form taken by God's holy laughter (verse 4) and wrath (verse 5), (a) in the Scriptures, and (b) in our contemporary history. What should be our attitude when confronted by modern-day oppressors?

3. Focus on the words of the king 'installed' by God (verses 7-9). They obviously applied originally to Israel's king (2 Samuel 7:14). God 'became' (i.e. was

publicly declared) the king's father on the day of coronation. When was Christ so acknowledged? Look up Hebrews 1:5 and Acts 13:32-33.

4. How should the expectations of verses 8 and 9 affect our prayer life? Note their messianic fulfilment in the New Testament (e.g. Revelation 12:5; 19:15).

5. In verses 10-12, list the human responses required by God's supreme King. Discuss them in the light of Christ's warnings in the Sermon on the Mount. (Matthew 7:24-27)

Study 6

Revelation 12:1-12, which comes at the centre of the book of Revelation, sets out for us the principle of God's victory over evil. It is a challenging passage, but shot through with encouragement. These questions may help towards your understanding of it.

1. In verses 1-6, whom do the three figures represent? Check scripture with scripture: 'the woman' (cf. Isaiah 26:17-18); 'the child' (cf. Acts 13:32-33); 'the dragon' (cf. Revelation 12:7; 20:2).

2. Can you think of some of the 'birth pangs' endured by the people of God before the birth of Jesus, involving conflict, journeyings, persecutions, etc. (e.g. Hebrews 11:32-40; Matthew 2:16-18)?

3. 'Snatched up' (verse 5) – a reference to Christ's triumphant ascension as the completion of his saving earthly ministry. How far are the subsequent fortunes of the woman typical of the church – i.e. oppressed, but intact, in the wilderness?

4. Look now at verses 7-12, another aspect of the same vision of victory. The key to the victory is 'the blood of the Lamb' (verse 11). What do we learn here about the kingdom, the power of the devil and the continuing conflict?

5. Try to describe the main themes running through this entire passage.

Part Four: Living the kingdom

In the light of Part Four of this book, we come now to two final studies, in which we look at two passages in the New Testament letters.

Study 7

In **1 Peter 2:4-12**, the apostle Peter is writing to citizens of heaven who are, nevertheless, 'scattered' as strangers throughout five provinces (1 Peter 1:1). They are facing great trials (1 Peter 4:12), but are possessors of an inheritance that is eternal (1 Peter 1:4). This passage focuses on the kingdom (the 'royal') people of God and the calling that is theirs. Use these questions, if they are helpful.

1. What truths are taught by these different descriptions of the Stone that is Christ ('rejected', 'chosen', 'precious', verses 4-8)? Compare Psalm 118:22; Isaiah 28:16; Acts 4:10-12.

2. From verses 4 and 5, try to describe, in your own words, what are the responsibilities of God's people as a spiritual house built around Christ? Compare with Romans 12:1.

3. Why is Christ a stone that causes some to 'stumble' (verse 8)? In what way has he been a stone of stumbling (a) to you, and (b) to people you know?

4. Look at verse 9. What do you learn from the fact that these are all collective titles of God's people?

5. 'Out of darkness into his wonderful light' (verse 9). In the light of this phrase, talk about our responsibility to be a sign of the kingdom to others. Compare your insights with Isaiah 9:2.

6. See verses 10-12. How morally different is the Christian fellowship today from modern secular society?

Study 8

Finally, we come to **Romans 8:18-27**. Just as you could entitle verses 1-4 of Romans 8 'the liberation of the Spirit', verses 5-11 'the life of the Spirit', and verses 12-17 'the assurance of the Spirit', so we could call verses 18-27 'the ache of the Spirit'. 'Suffering' and 'glory' (verse 18) are twinned here, as in so many other parts of the New Testament. The following questions may help this pattern of the kingdom of God to become better focused as you study this passage.

1. In the light of this passage what do you understand by the phrase 'the "already" and the "not yet"'?

2. Why should there be an 'ache' in the created order (verses 19-22)? Compare Genesis 3:17 and Isaiah 24:5. In what way do you feel yourself to be aching with nature?

3. How can it be said that we 'ache' from hope? See verses 23-25. How is this ache expressed in daily Christian living? How can we live with this tension? Compare Philippians 3:12-15, 20-21.

4. Discuss what it means to 'ache' in prayer (verses 26-27), when circumstances baffle us as to how to pray (e.g. Psalm 77:3-4). Are there instances when the believer is aware of the intercession, of the

wordless promptings, of the Holy Spirit helping us to pray?

5. What can we learn from the saints and heroes of old about pacing ourselves in the life of faith? Compare your findings with Hebrews 11:13.

Christian Focus Publications publishes biblically-accurate books for adults and children. The books in the adult range are published in three imprints.

Christian Heritage contains classic writings from the past.

Christian Focus contains popular works including biographies, commentaries, doctrine, and Christian living.

Mentor focuses on books written at a level suitable for Bible College and seminary students, pastors, and others; the imprint includes commentaries, doctrinal studies, examination of current issues, and church history.

For a free catalogue of all our titles, please write to

Christian Focus Publications Ltd,
Geanies House, Fearn, Tain,
Ross-shire, IV20 1TW, Great Britain

For details of our titles visit us on our web site:

http://www.christianfocus.com